Pass
Your Driving
Theory
Test

Pass
Your Driving
Theory
Test

Published by BSM
in association with
Virgin Publishing

First published in the UK in 1996 by
The British School of Motoring Ltd
81/87 Hartfield Road
Wimbledon
LONDON SW19 3TJ

The questions contained in this book are prepared by BSM
as illustrations of the type of questions which might be found
in the Theory Test papers.

Statistics have been sourced from The Department of Transport
Road Accidents in Great Britain, The Casualty Report and from the
Parliamentary Advisory Committee on Transport Safety (PACTS).

The traffic signs contained in this book are reproduced by
the kind permission of Her Majesty's Stationery Office.

ISBN 0 7535 0005 1

Text by the Product Development Team, British School of Motoring
Illustrations by Marc Lacey of The Visual Works
Design, typesetting and reprographics by Prima Creative Services
Printed and bound in Italy by Rotolito Lombarda S.p.A., Milan

Contents

Foreword

Driving is an enjoyable and useful lifetime experience which is why every year nearly a million new learner drivers take to the road, each one of them with one clear ambition. This ambition is almost certainly the same as yours – to pass their driving test first time.

Of course, there is no substitute for practical experience when learning to drive. The best way to gain this is by taking lessons with a good professional driving instructor who uses the most up-to-date teaching techniques in a modern, dual-controlled car. However, it has always been equally important to prepare for your driving lessons and, since the introduction of the Theory Test, this is doubly true.

Pass Your Driving Theory Test and its companion volume, *Pass Your Driving Test*, are the ideal books to help you do just that.

Pass Your Driving Theory Test has been developed to help you study and learn easily and enjoyably. Using a mixture of illustrations and text which talk to you just like your instructor, the book takes you through all the topics included in the Theory Test syllabus.

The book goes much further than simply presenting all the facts, figures and other knowledge you

To be a good driver it is important to learn about basic car maintenance.

need to pass your Theory Test successfully. It encourages you to participate in your learning and to think about the relevance of the information you need to know. You are invited to explore your own beliefs and attitudes and to try out your skills as an accident investigator. You are shown how to recognise common potential accident situations and how to master a set of habits to reduce risks. You will travel with the author on imaginary journeys round town, country and motorway roads and learn your road signs and

regulations as you go. You will learn the basics of car maintenance, and read about the documentation needed to drive, the safety equipment available in cars and the steps we all can take to preserve the environment.

There are no short cuts to becoming a safe and competent motorist, but that does not mean that you cannot enjoy yourself while learning. *Pass Your Driving Theory Test* will, I hope, bring the Theory Test alive and make it relevant, and at the same time it should also help you develop your driving skills.

In over 85 years of teaching people to drive, BSM instructors have helped millions of people pass their driving test. In my view, *Pass Your Driving Theory Test* and its companion volume, *Pass Your Driving Test,* are the best books available to help you make the most of your driving lessons and ensure that you prepare for both the theory and practical parts of your driving test in a structured and positive way.

Keith Cameron
Head of Road Safety Policy

Keith Cameron is one of Britain's leading authorities on motoring and driver education. He has held a number of senior positions within the Department of Transport; up to March 1992 he was Chief Driving Examiner with responsibility for all UK driving tests.

Introduction

You may well know somebody who has been driving for so long that they were never required to pass a driving test. They will almost certainly be a senior citizen since driving tests first became compulsory back in 1935. The first person to pass this new test was taught by The British School of Motoring and his name was Mr Beene. Since then, millions of people have passed their driving test and taken to the road, many taught by BSM instructors. In all that time, the driving test has hardly changed – at least, until the last few years. Reverse parking was introduced as a practical test exercise in 1991, and in 1995 the decision was made to introduce a separate written Theory Test.

I conducted an informal survey to find out how people feel about this, and the results are rather telling. Most qualified drivers think the Theory Test is an excellent idea and should be as hard as possible. Those drivers faced with passing this extra hurdle on their way to gaining the freedom of the road tended to moan: 'Why us, why now, it's not fair.'

However you feel about it, the Theory Test is probably here to stay. In order to become a qualified driver and obtain a full licence you must now pass the Theory as well as the Practical Test.

My aim in putting together this book is to try and make learning as easy as possible for you and to make what you learn meaningful, and I know my aim is shared by all my colleagues at BSM. Although I shall talk to you as 'I' all the time, I have drawn on the

Qualified drivers and learners disagree about the Theory Test...

As a part of the Practical Test, reverse parking was introduced in 1991. Subjects tested are covered in the companion to this book, **Pass Your Driving Test.**

collected wisdom of many of the best current and past BSM instructors in the country.

I hope you will find the illustrations colourful and fun, and that the step-by-step approach, which provides you with the knowledge and skills you need to be a safe driver, sets you on the right road to improving these skills after the test and remaining accident free.

Preparing for your test

The first part of the driving test is a written theory test of your knowledge and attitudes, and the second part is a practical test of your driving.

In this book, I shall focus on the Theory Test and all you need to know to pass it. A companion volume, *Pass Your Driving Test*, concentrates on each item on which you are tested during the practical examination.

What is tested on the Theory Test?

The Theory Test has been developed to satisfy European Community regulations. It has a specific syllabus containing eleven mandatory topics and three additional topics, only one of which is tested in each examination.

The list on the following page may seem daunting, but worry not. As you work through the book I will cover each of the topic areas in detail.

Car and Motorcycle Theory Test Topics

Before each heading below, you will see the code S1, S2, S3 or S4. This indicates in which of the four sections of this book you will find the topic covered.

MANDATORY TOPICS

S1 – Importance of alertness
Consideration, anticipation, observation, awareness, distraction, boredom.

S1 – Attitudes to other road users
Consideration, close following, courtesy, priority.

S1 – Knowledge of safe distances between vehicles, braking distances etc. (Conditions)
Safety margins and effect of bad weather and road surface conditions, visibility.

S1 – Impairment
Knowledge of reaction times and effects on driving behaviour of alcohol, fatigue, medication, drugs, stress, ill-health, ageing, sensory impairment (including eyesight).

S1 – Perception
Information processing, attention, scanning, identification of hazards, time to detect hazards, fixation, interpretation.

S1 – Judgement and decision-making
Appropriate action, interpretation, reaction time, speed, distance.

S2 – Risk factors associated with different road users
Children, pedestrians, disabled people, cyclists, elderly drivers, motorcyclists, new drivers/lack of traffic experience.

S2 – Risk factors associated with different road conditions
Own vehicle handling. Effects of: weather, road conditions, time of day (darkness), lighting, traffic calming, speed.

S2 – Behaviour in an accident
Rules on how to behave in case of an accident. Use of first aid kit and other first aid precautions, setting warning device and raising alarm, police reporting procedures, witness responsibilities, regulations.

S3 – Characteristics and statutory requirements of different types of roads
● Limitations on motorways: speed limits, lane discipline, stopping, lighting.
● Limitations on other types of road: speed limits, parking, clearways, lighting.

S3 – Road signs and traffic regulations
Road traffic regulations regarding road signs, markings, signals, rights of way and speed limits.

S4 – Administrative documents
Rules on administrative documents required for use of vehicles.

S4 – Safety factors relating to the vehicle and persons carried
Vehicle loading, stability, towing, regulations.

OPTIONAL TOPICS (Select one)

S4 – Mechanical aspects
How to detect the most common mechanical faults, defects that can affect safety, understanding of implications.

S4 – Vehicle safety equipment
Use of safety equipment (seat belts etc).

S4 – The environment
Rules on vehicle use in relation to the environment, emissions, fuel consumption, pollution (including noise), regulations.

Before Learning to Drive

Once you have decided you want to learn to drive, you probably can't wait to get started – and more to the point, you probably can't wait to pass your test. But before you can take to the road, there are a few things you must do if you want to stay legal, and I shall start by telling you about them.

The legal requirements

The minimum age at which you are allowed to drive a car on the public roads is 17, unless you are a disabled person in receipt of mobility allowance in which case the minimum age is 16. Until the day you pass the practical part of your driving test, you are not allowed to drive on your own. You must be accompanied by someone over 21 who has held a full British driving licence – valid for the type of vehicle you wish to drive – for a minimum of three years.

Before you start to drive or apply to take your Theory Test, you must obtain a provisional driving licence. You can get an application form, D1, from any BSM branch. You may not drive until you have actually received this first licence and signed it in ink.

Before driving, you must also check that:

- Your eyesight meets the minimum standard
- The vehicle you plan to drive is taxed, and the tax disc is displayed on the nearside (left) corner of the windscreen
- The vehicle is insured for you to drive and learn in
- If the vehicle is more than three years old, it has an MOT Certificate
- You have fixed L-plates of the regulation size to the vehicle so that they can be seen from front and rear (don't put L-plates in the windows where they will restrict your vision).

There is a minimum age for drivers...

Personal preparation

From July 1, 1996 the driving test is split into two parts: a written Theory Test of mainly multiple-choice questions, and a Practical Test of your driving. You must pass both parts before you can obtain a full driving licence. Until the end of 1996, you are allowed to take the two parts of the test in any order. But from January 1, 1997 you must pass the Theory Test before you are allowed to apply for the Practical Test.

No two people are the same and you must decide for yourself how you wish to go about your learning for both parts of the test. Some people prefer to get the theory under their belt first before starting driving lessons. That is fine, but for many people it feels too much like academic hard graft, because there is no chance to link the theory to the practice. Most people seem to find it easier to study theory and start driving lessons at the same time. The chance to put some of the theory into practice makes it feel more relevant and understandable.

If you study in this way at BSM, your instructor has a unique range of BSM materials and learning aids to hand, all designed to make learning as easy as possible for every type and age of pupil. Even if you have never passed an examination in your life or last studied 50 years ago, I am confident that with the right help you will be successful at the Theory Test. If you would like further information about the wide range of Theory Test services provided by BSM or would like help applying for a Theory Test, please call your local BSM branch on 0800 700 800.

How to use this book

I have taken the topics that you need to study and split them into four sections. In broad terms these are:

- You the driver
- Sharing the road with others
- The road (rules, regulations and road signs)
- Your vehicle.

Each section provides you with information, exercises to help you think, quizzes to test your knowledge, and example Theory Test questions.

While it is probably best to study the book in sequence, it is not a problem to dip in and out of any section you wish. Nobody remembers everything the first time they read it, see it or hear it, so don't be afraid to read something again or to try the exercises more than once.

Mock test papers are available from any BSM branch. If you have started practical lessons, your BSM instructor has been specially trained to guide you through your studies. If you need help you only have to ask.

The look and learn method

To make learning with this book more enjoyable and to help you remember what you have learnt, many drawings have been used. By studying the diagrams and their accompanying explanations, you will be able to understand easily the essential points and procedures you need to know to pass your driving test.

I hope the cartoon-style pictures will entertain you, but more importantly they are intended to help you remember the rules you must learn and the faults you must avoid.

The need for a professional driving instructor

The Driving Standards Agency strongly recommends that you take lessons from an Approved Driving Instructor (ADI), and there is no doubt that this is the best and the safest way to learn.

Anyone who gives car driving lessons for payment or reward must be registered with the Driving Standards Agency and they are required to display an ADI identification certificate on the windscreen of the tuition car. To become an ADI, you must pass examinations which are of a high standard.

The Highway Code

However well you study this book and any other materials you may obtain, it is essential that you read and understand the *Highway Code*. This is the official guide for all road users and an invaluable aid to road safety.

There seems no better way to get you started than to wish you **GOOD LUCK!** ∎

1. You the Driver

Attitudes and Beliefs

I sometimes wonder what life must have been like before the motor car was invented, and I wonder even more what life without cars would be like today. Cars provide us with enormous benefits but at financial, human and environmental cost. However, now you have started driving or are about to learn you will probably come to rely on your car as a necessary and essential means of transport. I know I certainly do, and any thought of going back to my days of waiting for buses in the wind and rain fills me with dread.

In a few weeks or months you may well have achieved your goal and passed your driving test. Meanwhile, my job in this book is to focus on the Theory Test and to make it as easy and enjoyable as possible for you to learn and pass.

But first I want to talk to you about attitudes to driving, both your attitude and that of others. I would like you to think about the following five statements and decide whether or not you agree with them. You may even wish to make a note of your response so that you can look back later and see if you still feel the same.

1. When I learn to drive, more attention should be paid to developing my attitude than to improving my handling of the car beyond a basic level of competence.
2. When I have passed my test, I shall not significantly reduce my risk of accident just by developing a high level of ability to control my car.
3. Regardless of my age, I stand a great risk of having an accident serious enough to involve an insurance claim within my first two years of driving.
4. When I drive, I can largely choose to remain accident free regardless of how other road users behave.
5. If I do have an accident, the odds are that I won't learn from my mistake and am likely to have another similar one.

You may have decided by now that only a madman could make such statements, let alone print them in a book, but I hope your curiosity will have been sufficiently aroused to make you want to read on.

What makes a good driver

The history of the motor car has some relevance to most people's beliefs about what makes a good driver. The first car was invented in 1885 by Carl Benz, and a strange contraption it was indeed. It ran on alcohol, and had three wheels like an old-fashioned invalid carriage.

For years after this, cars had mechanical brakes, non-synchromesh gears, tyres that didn't grip the road, steering that required the muscles of a weight-lifter to turn, and a suspension system that bounced you up and down like a yo-yo. These early cars coughed into life with a starting handle that could easily strain a wrist or break an arm. Once going, they were hard to control and even harder to stop.

In these early days not many people drove and those who did were looked upon as great adventurers, in the same way as early pilots and explorers were held in awe. As car ownership spread after World War II, learning to drive was largely seen as a need to master the beast that was the car and develop the physical skills needed to achieve this. A good driver was seen as one who could handle a car well and, as cars became able to go faster, a good driver simply changed to one who

The first cars were strange contraptions.

could handle a car well at high speed.

This belief has altered little and to this day affects the criteria on which you are tested. Even advanced driving tests place great emphasis on expert car control skills. You may not find this at all strange because you will probably agree that in order to conduct your journey safely you must be physically able to control the car. And yet cars are so much easier to handle now than they were all those years ago and very few people have much problem gaining a reasonable level of physical skill. It may be that the driving test has failed to keep pace with the changed nature of the driving task.

Advertising and the car

In varying degrees, nearly all of us have some sort of love affair with our cars. We wash and polish them, sometimes give them names and treat them almost as one of the family. Your car is likely to be much more to you than simply a box on wheels to take you from A to B.

Many of our attitudes and beliefs about cars and driving come from being bombarded by messages from the car industry. Car manufacturers sell their products by presenting us with exciting images designed to grab our attention. That's their job and they do it very successfully through advertising. Since we all watch TV and read magazines, these images settle in our brain even if we're not that bothered about buying a car.

Cars, you are persuaded, can make you whatever you want to be, and make others see you as you wish to be seen. An exciting car will make you an exciting person, give you status, improve your sex life and give you freedom. Because cars are packed full of safety features such as seat belts, impact bars, air-bags and collapsible steering columns

POLISH   PREEN

LOVE

The car is often the most pampered member of the family.

you believe you have the freedom to speed and to take risks. You believe you won't get hurt if you have an accident because only a person as skilled as you can keep the car under control. We know that all this is exaggerated nonsense, but the images are powerful and many of us are taken in by them. Some of us have accidents as a result of such images.

Academic research

Each year an enormous amount of research is conducted into the causes of road accidents by countries all over the world. In England, for example, the Transport Research Laboratory and several universities – including Reading, Birmingham and Southampton – are at the forefront of research in the field. As you might expect, every country seems to have a road accident problem, though some have a better record than others. What you may not know is that over the last few years research findings from many countries around the world have highlighted that:

■ If you have an accident, your level of car control ability is unlikely to have been the cause

■ Statistically, those people who undertake further training in car

You believe that you are the only person who can control the beast.

control skills – including handling the car at speed, in simulated emergency situations and in adverse conditions – remain just as likely to be involved in a crash as drivers who have no such training.

And yet nearly everyone believes that increased skills-based training makes drivers safer, that you will be able to get out of dangerous situations more easily, and that your superior driving skills will help you avoid emergency situations in the first place.

In addition, it is widely assumed that by learning and mastering advanced driving skills your attitude and behaviour will be changed and you will become a safer driver.

Research, I'm afraid, suggests that just teaching advanced car control training may actually make you more likely to be involved in an accident, rather than less. Nobody is quite sure why this should be the case, though misplaced confidence may be the cause.

Developing your driving skills

When you learn to drive, particularly in the early stages, you are likely to find that physically controlling the car takes up nearly all your attention. Steering, gear changing, clutch control, smooth acceleration, braking and so forth all seem a lot to do. While most people won't remember they failed to see a pedestrian crossing the road, and nearly ran them over on a driving lesson, they will certainly recall car control problems such as the occasions when they stalled several times at a set of traffic lights, the lights turned back to red and a queue of impatient drivers was kept waiting behind.

Too few driving lessons and too little practice often means that your car control skills may still be less than adequate on the day you pass your test. Although virtually everybody can learn to drive, regardless of mental or physical ability, roughly 50 per cent of people taking tests fail. Those who pass do so because they drive for about 30 minutes without revealing any potentially or actually dangerous faults. They may have attitude problems, but will still pass, because the driving test cannot really assess attitude and only a complete idiot would deliberately commit anti-social behaviour with the examiner sitting in the car. As soon as the pass certificate is received and the examiner is out of the way, however, devil horns may start to grow.

Once you have passed your test, even with no further formal training your ability to control the car is likely to improve significantly simply through practice. The skill and accuracy with which you now handle your car is likely to make you believe that you are a good driver. If you *are* a good driver this will be because you feel it important to drive safely and you reflect this in your behaviour by taking fewer risks. However, your increased confidence can adversely affect your behaviour as a driver, encouraging you to take more risks and increasing the chances of an accident happening.

A while ago I listened to a group of young drivers informally discussing cars and driving and here are some of their comments. Will you think like this when you've passed your test and if not, why not?

- 'I'm a good driver now because I no longer drive like a learner.'
- 'Everyone else on the road is an idiot except me.'
- 'I can take risks that other drivers should avoid, because I'm better.'
- 'Other people have accidents.'
- 'I am safe, my car is safe and I expect everyone else to be like me and get it right all the time. When they don't I get aggressive.'
- 'I want to get there quickly. I drive up people's exhaust pipes to make them move over. I drive at a safe speed – fast. Of course I can stop, my reactions are superb.'
- 'I am brilliant at judging distance.'
- 'I am brilliant at judging speed and space.'
- 'My timing is faultless; I can change lanes and slip into the smallest gap with ease.'
- 'My concentration is so good I don't have to think about driving. It's become natural and I can think about other things while I drive.'

If you agree with these statements, you are not alone. In late 1995, a research survey – conducted by MORI on behalf of BSM – showed that 99 per cent of those surveyed rated their own driving skills as above average while 26 per cent believed they had no bad driving habits at all. Yet they could all provide a long list of other people's bad driving habits.

Road accident statistics – over 3,500 people dead and over 300,000 people injured on our roads each year – show how we delude ourselves and

'My concentration is so good I don't have to think about driving.'

Poor driving contributes to 3,500 people dead and over 300,000 injured each year.

overrate our driving abilities.

We fail to recognise that our bad driving habits contribute to causing accidents. Although we believe other people driving aggressively or speeding are likely to be involved in an accident, we believe our own skill will keep us safe when we choose to drive dangerously. But skill, or the lack of it, is not the major factor that causes accidents. It is our attitude or behaviour – and this you *can* choose. So you can choose to be aggressive, you can choose to drive too fast, to cut people up, drive up their exhaust pipe, overtake on the left and so on. In effect, you can choose whether to risk having an accident.

If you do have an accident, statistics indicate that your chances of having a similar one in the next three years are doubled. If you were partly responsible for the accident, you are four times more likely to be involved in a similar one within the next year. This is because your behaviour will remain unchanged if you seriously believe you did not help to cause the accident.

I shall return to common accidents and their causes later in this book.

At this stage, you may wish to glance back at the five statements I asked you to consider on page 14. I have started the process of trying to let you see their significance, and I shall reinforce that process throughout this book.

Vision and Perception

In the previous pages I am not attempting to suggest that the way you drive is exclusively governed by your beliefs and attitudes, although they certainly play a major part. How you think and feel significantly affects the way you behave when you drive. But safe driving involves other factors as well, and is a combination of your physical skills, your knowledge and your attitude.

Let me offer you an example. Imagine you are driving down a road and you see a junction ahead and a Give Way sign.

If you do not know what a Give Way sign means you clearly have a knowledge problem and may cause an accident. If you know what the sign means, but cannot physically control your car to slow down or stop if necessary, you have a skills problem and may still cause an accident.

Even if you can physically control your car, you may still choose to break the rules, pull out of the junction regardless,

and cause another vehicle to slow down, swerve or stop. In this case your problem would be either poor judgement, or an attitude that lets you feel such risky behaviour is acceptable.

So once you have mastered the basic physical skills and knowledge, safe driving has far more to do with what is going on in your head than what you are doing with your hands and feet.

To drive safely you need to think and act decisively. To do that you need information. To get information you first have to look. Actually, you have to do more than look. You have to see. Seeing is more than looking

because seeing makes sense of what you look at. That is what is meant by perception. Let me explain to you some things about vision and perception.

Your eyesight

Advances in modern technology mean that most people can learn to drive and pass a driving test regardless of their physical disabilities. But while cars can be specially adapted to the disabled there is unfortunately no such help available for partially sighted people, unless glasses or contact lenses will do the trick.

Good eyesight is essential for safe driving. When you take the practical part of your driving test, the examiner will check that your eyesight meets the minimum legal standard by asking you to read a car number plate from a distance of at least 20.5 metres (67 feet). You are allowed to wear glasses or contact lenses if necessary, but if you have any doubts about your ability to meet the eyesight requirements easily, seek advice from an optician before you start to drive; and in any case remember to have your eyesight checked regularly by an optician.

Please note that it is illegal to drive a car if you cannot pass the eyesight test; and remember that if you need to wear glasses or contact lenses to read the number plate on your test, you

A cold can ruin your concentration and it may be better not to drive if you feel unwell.

must continue to wear them the whole of the time you are driving.

There are several other factors that can contribute towards how well you can see and concentrate.

After the age of 40 or so eyesight tends to deteriorate. The biggest danger is that the deterioration is usually so gradual that it is hard to detect the change.

Other people have what is called 'night blindness' which can make it difficult to discern objects easily in low light. This can be detected on a simple eyesight check.

Tiredness also affects your ability to see properly and to drive competently. You need to be prepared to pull up somewhere safe and legal and have a break from driving. Take a catnap or a stroll and refreshments before resuming the drive. Stress can affect you in a similar way.

Even a cold can disturb your concentration, and if you are feeling unwell it might be better not to drive at all. If you do have to drive, take things slower than usual, as this will give you more time to react.

It is of course illegal to drive if you have been drinking and are over the legal limit, which is 35microgrammes per 100 millilitres of breath. It can be difficult to judge what you are allowed to drink while remaining within the limit and, since evidence suggests that reactions are slowed down after just one glass of wine, it is best to remain stone-cold sober.

Medication often causes drowsiness – in which case you shouldn't drive. So check your medicine bottle carefully and, if you are still unsure, ask a pharmacist or doctor.

Do note, moreover, that it is illegal to drive under the influence of drugs.

If you are suffering from shock or bereavement your ability to concentrate can be turned upside down for days and it is probably best to avoid driving completely in these circumstances.

And do remember that the driver in front or behind could be feeling less than 100 per cent themselves. So take care.

Looking and seeing

Let's suppose you have had your eyes checked, and now know whether or not you need glasses for driving. Yet still your eyes are not as accurate as you think they are. Nor are mine. Nor are anybody else's. As your eyes scan the printed matter on this page, for instance, you will automatically read the printed matter as words, not merely as a pattern of marks on a white surface. We do this all the time: we don't simply see, we read. And when it comes to driving, we need to learn to read the road. The problem, however, is that we can easily misread a road just as we can when reading a page. Let me illustrate what I mean. Read the sentence below, just once, and count the number of **F**s in the sentence.

FINISHED FILES ARE THE RESULT OF YEARS OF SCIENTIFIC STUDY COMBINED WITH THE EXPERIENCE OF MANY YEARS.

I have asked many people to read this sentence and in a group of 10 or 12 it would be unusual for more than two to find six **F**s the first time they read it. Often people miss the **F** in the middle of SCIENTIFIC because they recognise the word and understand it without needing to look at each individual letter. Often they miss the **F**s at the end of the 'ofs' because of the 'v' sound.

Basically, we read for meaning. Unless we are professional proof-readers, we don't read every single letter of every single word of every single sentence.

And often our eyes are not as accurate as we think they are and they can catch us out. This can cause huge

problems when driving because everyone sees things differently. Take a look at this optical illusion.

Do you see an Eskimo or an Indian head? Either the shaded area on the right is the opening to an igloo with an Eskimo facing inwards, or the shaded area is an Indian's head-dress, the Eskimo's arm the Indian's ear. In any case, it is possible to find both.

Let me point out a number of relevant things about this image:

1. Once you have learned how to see both figures you will not forget.
2. Once you have learned where both figures are you will find your eyes automatically slip from one to the other.

3. You cannot see both images at the same time.
4. Both images are equally good. Neither dominates the other, even if you originally thought there was only one figure in the picture.

This image illustrates how we see and perceive things when driving. It shows us how our eyes allow us to interpret information. The point I am making is that if, when driving along, you see things differently from someone else you have a problem.

The background, for instance, affects the way we see things. Look at this drawing:

In this illusion both inner circles are the same size, yet the inner circle on the left appears bigger because the surrounding dots are smaller. When driving, background affects the way we judge distance, speed and size. In the case of motorways – deliberately featureless so as to provide as few distractions as possible – lack of background makes it extremely difficult to judge the speed we are travelling at or the speed of other vehicles. This is why it is advisable, when leaving the motorway, to check the speedometer: you are likely to be travelling much faster than you think. Similarly, on a 30mph stretch of road with cars parked on both sides 30mph can feel very fast; yet on a wide road with no parked cars 30mph would feel extremely slow.

We often see what we expect to see, and this gives rise to problems when roads are changed. When mini-roundabouts were first introduced, some drivers drove straight over them. If there had been a crossroads there before, and they were accustomed to driving through (past the side roads) they had ceased to register the presence of a junction. Unfamiliarity was another problem: many drivers simply didn't know what a mini-roundabout was – the better ones were slowed by their confusion, others simply ignored it.

A similar response can be seen when traffic lights fail and are switched off. If the light is neither red nor amber, some drivers will nonetheless register green and go straight through without checking.

Take a look at the picture below and see how many things you can identify that you wouldn't normally expect to see.

Did you notice the pumpkin or the upside-down cat in the tree, the crescent moon, the key in the door pillar, the witch's face on the path and

the witch's broom on the fence?

When driving it is often the unexpected in the picture that catches you out and causes the accident. You might imagine you would be safest driving closest to home because you are familiar with the roads. However, it is precisely this familiarity that can cause the problem. I know someone who drove the same route to work every day. He always cut a corner at a particular junction, until the unexpected caught him out and he hit a car emerging as he turned into the road. There had never been anyone there before and he was taken by surprise.

The problem, however, is that you can never see everything.

The picture below is a variation of Kim's Game, a memory game I played as a child. Study the picture for five seconds and then, without cheating, answer the questions on the following page. Then look at the picture again and check your answers on page 29.

Kim's Game questions

1. Was it raining?
2. What vehicle(s) was/were visible in the mirror?
3. Where was the van parked?
4. What was the car ahead doing?
5. What was special about the car signalling right?
6. Where was the skateboarder?
7. Where was the pedestrian with the dog?
8. Describe who was on the pedestrian crossing?
9. What vehicle was on the far side of the crossing?
10. What time was it?
11. What colour was the car ahead?
12. What number was the bus?
13. Did the crossing have a central refuge?
14. Which way did the road go after the pedestrian crossing?

You have probably discovered that you can't see everything. And of course, when driving you wouldn't normally have anything like five seconds to study the road. The scene changes constantly and, in trying to see everything, you miss the details. To answer the questions, you probably had to do a certain amount of guesswork. You might, for example, have seen a car ahead but not its colour, or a bus but not the number. You may have noted the crossing but not whether there was a central refuge. Many of these details are largely irrelevant anyway. The important thing is to select what it is important to see, not to focus on the details and try to see everything.

Perception is more than having your eyes open and your head pointed in the right direction. You must make

Avoid common distractions, such as changing a tape or CD while driving.

sense of what you see and act accordingly. Reading the road involves interpreting what you see, not just seeing what is there. Our ability to take in visual information from a scene is limited, which puts a premium on concentration when driving. If you become distracted, you may miss a vital piece of information through focusing your attention elsewhere. You must know what you are looking for or you will not take everything in. So just consider some of these common distractions and how easy it is to allow them to disrupt your concentration:

■ Advertising hoardings and scenery
■ Changing a tape, trying to read a map or peering at nameplates of streets
■ Worrying about something
■ Hurrying because you are late for an appointment.

When driving, your brain is already working overtime. Not only do you need to see what is there and make sense of it, but equally importantly you have to work out what is going to happen next. Anticipation calls for imagination so that we can transform what we see. We must ask ourselves: 'What if?' Imagination allows us to play

Kim's Game answers

1. Yes, it was raining – you can see umbrellas, and the road and pavements are shiny with the wet
2. A brown car and a motorcyclist
3. The van was parked illegally, on zigzag lines and half over the pavement
4. The car ahead was braking
5. The driver was a learner
6. Coming out from behind the parked lorry on the right
7. Standing on the right-hand pavement at the zebra crossing
8. A woman pushing a baby carriage was on the pedestrian crossing
9. There was a bus on the far side of the pedestrian crossing
10. The time was 3:30
11. Green
12. The bus was a number 28
13. Yes, there was a central refuge
14. The road curved to the left after the pedestrian crossing

out different responses to various scenarios before an event actually occurs. The earlier we start to solve problems, the more options we have. You may not be able to look round corners but you can see round them in your imagination.

So far I have considered how to look, select, see and interpret. The purpose of all this hard work is to enable you to make decisions and then act on them.

Judgements and Decision-Making

Before you can safely decide what action you should take, you need to be able to judge the situation accurately. In driving, one of the most difficult things I can remember learning was how to judge a safe gap when emerging onto a busy road.

Imagine the following scenario. You are driving along in the middle lane of a three-lane motorway, closing on the car in the left-hand lane and you will shortly be overtaking it. Up ahead of the car in the left lane is a lorry that the car is gaining on.

You need to imagine what will happen if the car pulls out to overtake the lorry. What if you are alongside the car when the driver pulls out?

What if you are being overtaken at the same time by a car in the outside lane? A number of unpleasant scenarios are possible, and you must find ways to transform the situation.

Check whether the outside lane is free for you to pull into. Estimate whether you can get up to – and past – the car ahead well before it reaches the lorry. Work out how much you need to slow down to hold back from the car long enough to tell whether the driver will remain behind the lorry. You may change lane, or you may give a long headlamp flash to warn of your presence.

This scenario should be running through your head, even though you may not act on any of it. Try to keep your options open for as long as

In any potentially hazardous situation you should be running 'what if' scenarios.

When road conditions are icy, stopping distances can easily increase tenfold.

possible. But leave a decision too late and you'll find there's a car in the outside lane, and the driver of the car in the left lane is unaware of your presence. Then you'll find yourself either involved in an accident or having to brake suddenly.

So in the end you have to do something. There are really only three things you can do:

- Speed up (accelerate)
- Slow down (brake)
- Change direction (steer).

The time it takes to make your decision affects the speed at which you should be travelling. In other words, you may well need to be slowing down to give yourself time to decide on an appropriate course of action and time to react.

Experiments have shown that experienced drivers tend to react to danger earlier than a new driver. But experienced drivers do not necessarily have quicker reactions. Their past experience simply helps them spot danger earlier and start to react earlier. If you know and have learned all about reaction times and how long it takes a car to stop in theory, you have already gained valuable and crucial experience before you even start thinking about taking your driving test.

So let me tell you about overall stopping distances.

We established earlier that you

can't react to a problem until you have spotted it. So as a general guide, the more there is to think about, the slower you should be going. This gives you time to brake which cannot be done in an instant.

The overall stopping distance is governed by:

- Reaction times
- Braking distances.

The overall stopping distance is the distance your car will travel from the moment you recognise the need to brake to the moment your car stops.

Your reaction time will vary depending on your physical and mental well-being. If you are tired, ill, suffering from shock or on medication, your ability to react will be impaired. And even if you are in the best of health it will take at least half a second to react

and decide to brake. The distance you cover in this time will increase by roughly one third of a metre (or one foot) for every mile per hour of speed. At 30mph you will therefore travel 9 metres or 30 feet before your foot even touches the brake.

At 30mph it will take you another 14 metres (45 feet) to stop the car in addition to this reaction distance.

Have a look at the chart below. From it, you will notice that if you double your speed, let's say from 30mph to 60mph, your braking distance actually quadruples, from 14 to 55 metres.

These distances are minimum overall stopping distances. If the road surface is wet, the time it will take you to stop will be doubled. If the road surface is icy, it can take you up to ten times as long to stop.

Not only must you know your

speed	thinking distance	braking distance	overall stopping distance
20mph	6m / 20ft	6m / 20ft	12m / 40ft
30mph	9m / 30ft	14m / 45ft	23m / 75ft
40mph	12m / 40ft	24m / 80ft	36m / 120ft
50mph	15m / 50ft	38m / 125ft	53m / 175ft
60mph	18m / 60ft	55m / 180ft	73m / 240ft
70mph	21m / 70ft	75m / 245ft	96m / 315ft

Try striding towards a lamp post to check your estimate of its distance.

to be able to judge your stopping distances, as summed up by rule 57 of the *Highway Code*:

> Drive at a speed that will allow you to stop well within the distance you can see to be clear.
> Leave enough space between you and the vehicle in front so that you can pull up safely if it suddenly slows down or stops.

When it comes to separation distances, the safest gap to leave between you and the vehicle in front is your overall stopping distance. At 20mph you should leave a gap of 12 metres or 40 feet – roughly equivalent to three car lengths. At 30mph you should leave a gap of 23 metres or 75 feet – or six car lengths.

overall stopping distances, you must also be able to judge them. You can practise this as a pedestrian by picking a lamp post and guessing how far away it is. Then check your estimate by striding towards it, one good stride roughly equalling a metre (or a yard). Try this out on other objects until you get accurate at it.

There are two reasons for needing

After about 40mph it becomes extremely difficult to judge distances, so we use what is known as the two-second rule. When the vehicle in front of you passes a stationary object such as a road sign, you say: 'A thousand and one. A thousand and two,' or 'Only a fool breaks the two-second rule.' This takes two seconds to say, so if you pass the road sign before you've finished counting you are too close to the vehicle in front. A car covers one and a half feet per second per mile per hour of speed. In other words, the distance that your car travels over the road is one and a half times the speed at which you are driving.

At 40mph this is 60 feet (1.5 x 40), at 50mph it is 75 feet, and so on. To get the distance travelled for two seconds you simply double these distances so that 60 feet becomes 120 feet, 75 feet becomes 150 feet.

This is not an exact science. For instance, if you do the calculation for 30mph over two seconds, you will have travelled 90 feet, which is in fact 15 feet more than the overall stopping distance shown on page 32. In any case, it is safer to observe the two-second rule, even at lower speeds, than to underestimate the gap you need to leave.

In heavy traffic it is not always practical to leave your overall stopping distance at slow speeds, so you may close the gap. You should never get any closer than your reaction distance (one foot per mph of speed) because if the vehicle in front has to stop suddenly, you wouldn't have enough room between you and it to stop safely.

You must also consider the prevailing conditions. If it's raining or foggy or other vehicles are throwing up surface spray, you need to leave double your distance – i.e. a four-second time gap. After a long hot spell oil and grease build up on the roads and the first drops of rain can put your car at risk of aquaplaning (sliding across the surface of the road because the tyres can't get a grip through the grease).

In the end, this all comes back to attitude. Despite knowing about overall stopping distances and how to apply the two-second rule, some motorists still drive ridiculously close to one another, because they choose to ignore what they know.

Even knowing the dangers, some motorists still follow too closely together.

Learning to See

I mentioned earlier that regardless of age, you are at far greater risk of an accident during your first two years of driving than at any other time.

I also explained some of the problems our eyes and brain cause us when we are driving and how they are liable to deceive us. Since we cannot take everything in – we can easily miss seeing things or misinterpret what we do see – we need to learn how to select what it is important to see and we must also use our imagination to predict what might happen next.

It is clear that part of this 'seeing' ability – sometimes described as awareness and anticipation – comes with experience which explains in part why inexperienced drivers have more accidents. Interestingly, research seems to confirm this. Newly-qualified drivers spot fewer problems, and see problems later than more experienced drivers, so that the possibility of an accident is obviously greater. Most new drivers are young, and some young drivers tend to drive erratically. They drive too fast and brake too late and too harshly. Their aggressive, risk-taking behaviour is caused by undeveloped perception skills as much as by a bad attitude.

A mixture of research, experiment and analysis of the results of training methods reveals two things.

First, advanced car control training reduces experienced drivers' accident rates much less dramatically than more sophisticated attempts to alter their

Young drivers are often blamed for fast, erratic driving.

beliefs and behaviour, and develop their risk awareness. For example, BSM Qualified Driver Training Ltd has achieved remarkable reductions in the accident rates of fleet drivers. Such training costs money, but reduced accidents mean lower insurance premiums and less time off work, and companies who undertake such training can save money as well as lives.

Secondly, inexperienced drivers – even pre-drivers under 17 – appear to be able to learn and develop perception skills through specialist training rather than through a process of trial and error while actually driving.

BSM uses in-car commentary driving techniques to help develop this mental process, based on research carried out by the Transport Research Laboratory (or TRL).

BSM has also developed a training system for all newly-qualified drivers and potential drivers which teaches selective perception skills normally gained through experience.

Drivers learn to put into practice five simple habits which, when used together, enable you to acquire the 'seeing eye' of an experienced motorist. These Five Habits will help you to identify risks and then respond to them. I must stress that these habits have very little to do with your hands

Experienced drivers' accident rates can be lowered through influencing their beliefs and changing their behaviour.

and feet and your physical control of the car – however necessary these may be – and everything to do with linking what is going on inside your head with what is happening on the road. They are all about reading the road, showing awareness and being selective.

The Five Habits
You should find these habits straightforward and readily understandable, since you already make use of them in everyday life.

1. Look well ahead
2. Move your eyes
3. Spot the problems
4. Keep space
5. Be seen

They are simple, like many of the best ideas in life – easy to take on board because they make sense, and easy to use if you work at them a bit. Habits, by their very nature, need to be developed and used continuously, particularly if they are going to work for you and keep you safe.

Now let's look at each one in turn.

1. Look well ahead

To some degree we all have to look well ahead in order to plan our lives and prevent them becoming chaotic. You may be looking ahead to a rock concert months away – fail to buy the tickets early enough and you may be disappointed – or you may be planning for your retirement and be thinking about your pension.

Equally, it is fairly obvious that you need to look ahead when driving. If you stare down at the end of the bonnet you will find it impossible to steer your car in a straight line. If you fail to look where you are going you will be in danger of hitting something or driving off the road.

It may be useful to think of your eyes as the headlights of a car; headlights shine much further ahead on full beam than they do when dipped and angled towards the road, and similarly keeping your head up and your eyes high helps you to look well ahead. It is perhaps harder to decide how far ahead you need to be looking. Simply looking at the car in front is insufficient. You need to look as far beyond it as you can in order to give yourself time to plan your actions. This may be the horizon on a motorway, or closer on other roads where the road ahead disappears round a bend or over a hill. In town, junctions, buildings, other traffic, even pedestrians may drastically reduce the distance you can see in front.

Think of your eyes like the headlights of a car. When they are dipped they see this far:

On full beam they see much further ahead.

Looking well ahead allows you to plan early; the more time you have, the more options you have. Efficient planning leads to good timing, resulting in smooth, seemingly effortless performance.

Even if there is no other traffic on the road, it is important to look well ahead. Many accidents – especially for the 17 to 20-year-old age group – do not involve any other car or pedestrian. Steering smoothly and progressively keeps your car stable; and the faster you are driving, the further ahead you will need to look to find your steering path.

Unless you are looking well ahead, you have no means to decide a safe and sensible speed at which to drive. To make swift progress safely, you need to speed up and down at the right times. If you are too late slowing down, you may enter a corner too fast. If you are too late speeding up, you may miss an overtaking opportunity. Looking well ahead allows you time to anticipate a change of speed or course.

Let's now look at two examples where failing to look ahead could cause you problems.

In each of the diagrams on pages 39 and 40, imagine you are driving the red car. You are not looking far enough ahead; the orange-dotted area of the diagram shows you where you are looking.

In each case, you are missing one or more vital pieces of information that could have warned you to slow down. Try to identify these by looking at the diagram, then read the explanation below the diagram.

Many accidents in the teenage group don't even involve anyone else.

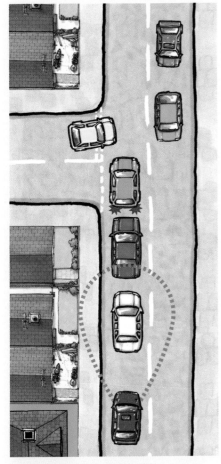 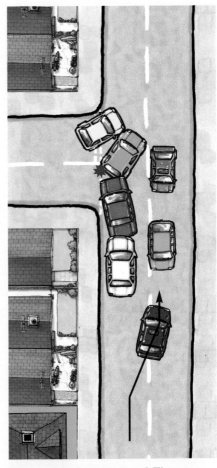

You didn't notice the junction on the left. The yellow car pulling out should have given way but didn't, and you failed to see it anyway. Nor did you notice that the green car is braking, as you didn't see the brake lights, nor were you aware that the cars in front are driving too close together.

What might happen next? The green car may hit the emerging yellow car and the cars behind might then pile into each other. You could do the same, unless you decided to avoid the collision by swerving to the right – which would take you straight into the path of oncoming traffic.

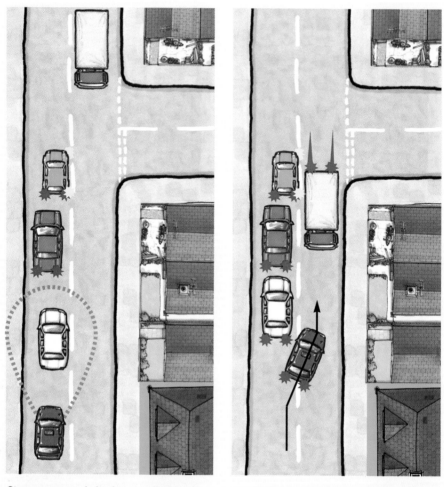

Since you aren't looking well ahead, you fail to notice that the green car is signalling right. You see neither the junction on the right, nor the green car's brake lights as it stops for the oncoming traffic. Closer to home, you have yet to notice the brake lights of the blue car or the fact that there is too little space to get past the green car as it waits for a safe gap.

What might happen next? The green car will have to wait for the lorry, so the blue car will stop. The white car in front of you will brake hard and also stop. You will probably either hit it or have to swerve dangerously.

2. Move your eyes

It is very important when driving to keep moving your eyes all the time. As you drive along, you need to picture everything that is happening 360° around your car. The picture changes every second or two, which means your information is in continual need of updating. But however good your eyesight may be, your eyes can only see objects clearly in a narrow cone of central vision – about 3° wide. This is simply the way our eyes are made. Take a look at Figure 1 and Figure 2 below, to see how this narrow cone of vision affects what we see while we are driving along.

Despite our narrow cone of central vision, we are still conscious of movement to either side. By moving our eyes and our head, we can focus clearly on the objects we have seen moving in our peripheral vision.

And, of course, we use the mirrors to look behind us. These don't show the whole picture, however, and at times you must turn your head to see into the areas of blind spot. If you turn your head to check these blind spots when the car is moving it can only be a quick glance, otherwise your steering may be affected or you might miss something ahead.

Figure 3 (over the page) shows the driver's view in the door mirror – it looks clear. But Figure 4 shows what's really happening in the driver's blind spot, while Figure 5 reveals how the situation appears when viewed from overhead.

Figure 1: The driver is looking well ahead. The central clear area is what is in focus. The rest of the picture shows what the driver detects in fringe vision.

Figure 2: The driver has moved his eyes to identify what was detected as moving in Figure 1, and focuses on the child running out.

Figure 3: In the driver's door mirror, the road behind appears to be clear.

Figure 4: But a turn of the head reveals an overtaking car in the driver's blind spot.

Figure 5: Because the red car is neither visible in the door mirror nor in the driver's normal 180°-forward vision, it is in the blind spot.

Moving your eyes also helps you stay alert. If you fix your eyes on one thing for more than a second or two, they develop a blank stare and the edges of your vision will become blurred. If you find you can't keep your eyes moving, you are almost certainly tired and in need of a rest.

So let's look at two more examples on the opposite page, Figures 6 and 7,

where failing to move your eyes might cause problems. Once again I'd like you to imagine that you are driving the red car. The orange-dotted area shows where you are focusing your eyes.

In each case, you will miss important information and encounter problems if you don't move your eyes often enough. Try to identify what you have missed, then read the explanation below each diagram.

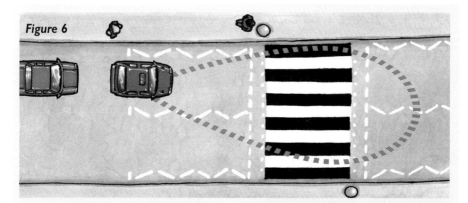

Figure 6

You are looking ahead, and have seen that the crossing is clear. But since you haven't moved your eyes to the sides and taken in the pavement, you have failed to notice the pedestrian on the left approaching the crossing. If the pedestrian reaches the crossing before you and decides to cross, you will have to brake hard and even then may not be able to stop in time. The car behind may also be caught unawares and end up hitting you from the rear.

Figure 7

The parked cars force the blue car onto the wrong side of the road. In the red car, you are looking to the right – the direction from which you would normally expect to see cars approaching. The road is clear, but because you don't look to your left, you fail to see the blue car and if you keep moving you may hit it. Even if you do look and see the problem, if you've already moved out you'll be blocking the road by the time you stop. Somebody will have to reverse which may not be easy if the blue car and those cars behind you have kept moving.

3. Spot the problems

It is the case with driving, as with so many things in life, that we can usually prevent a problem arising if we can see it coming.

This is why it is so important to look well ahead and keep your eyes moving, deciding where the problem areas might be. This way nothing will ever take you by surprise and your chances of having an accident are greatly reduced.

Take a look at the examples on these pages. In each case imagine that you are in the left-hand lane, driving into the diagram from the bottom (the illustration representing what you can see in front of you).

In Zone A the green pelican light might change. The parked van hides the left-hand pavement and will force you to change direction.

In Zone B you will be forced very near the centre line.

In Zone C the motorbike may overtake the car, leaving little space for you.

And in Zone D the pedestrian is pushing the button so the lights may change at any moment.

If you only had one problem to contend with you might be fine. It's the fact you have to take several into consideration that complicates the situation. If the motorcyclist weren't there you could pass the van, checking to the left for pedestrians.

As it is, you have to assess the size of the gap, ascertain whether the motorcyclist will allow you through, and remember to watch out for any concealed pedestrians.

Each diagram is split into four zones: A, B, C and D. Look at each zone to see if you can spot a problem, then read the explanation.

Here are more examples of potential problems you must spot:

■ Watch out for cars waiting to emerge from side roads. Has the driver looked your way? Will he wait or should you slow down in case he pulls out in front of you?

■ Is the driver of that parked car going to get out, opening the door right in front of you? Or is the driver planning to move off and, if so, will he turn round and check his blind spot?

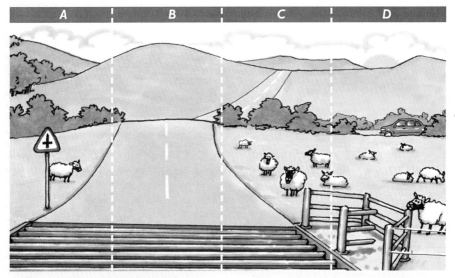

In *Zone A* *the cattle grid, the sheep and the crossroads ahead are the problems.*

In *Zone B* *the brow of the hill restricts your vision.*

In *Zone C* *the sheep may cross the road.*

In *Zone D* *the car may pull out in a dip ahead at the crossroads,* *and the sun may dazzle you.*

This diagram is in stark contrast to the one on the previous page and, at first glance, you might think you will encounter fewer problems in the countryside. However, as you can see, if you don't look well ahead and move your eyes constantly you could easily miss something.

- Is the dog on a lead?
- Can you see exhaust fumes from a parked car which might mean the driver is about to pull away?
- What if there is a lorry broken down around the bend?

All these examples put you at risk, but you can eliminate the danger if you spot it early enough.

4. Keep space

The problem with space in general is that there is only so much available and we have to share it with others. The more motorways and roads we build, the more cars and lorries seem to fill them. So trying to keep space around your car on today's roads is no easy matter. We need to achieve a delicate balance between keeping pace with traffic and keeping space from traffic. Space around your car gives you time to look, assess the dangers and then react to them. This space gives you an escape route if anything goes wrong or another driver makes a mistake. Obviously, the smaller the space, the greater the risk. And remember too, that too little space often causes aggression.

Small adjustments to your speed – by easing off the accelerator or covering the brake – allow you to approach hazards with care, and keep the safest possible position relative to other traffic on the road.

When driving you only have three options or means of escaping from a dangerous situation: you can change speed, you can change position or you

With everyone trying to snatch it, keeping space around you is no easy matter.

can give a warning signal. Keeping a proper distance gives you the chance to keep all your options open as long as possible.

Now let's look at some examples. Look at Figures 8 and 9 below, and imagine you are driving the red car. Ask yourself why one situation is safer than the other, and then read the explanation in the caption.

Although traffic will generally move into the spaces you leave, it is possible to widen the gap again by easing off the power. You may feel you're going to arrive at your destination much later but, believe me, the time lost is negligible. You may also become irritated if other drivers keep invading the spaces you are leaving, and you may be tempted to close up the gap so this doesn't happen. But remember that doing so increases your risk of an accident quite significantly.

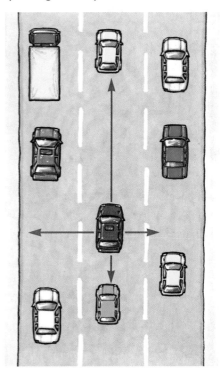

Figure 9: This is how a driver can create some space even in congested traffic. The red car now has space in which to slow or stop, and a space on the left to move into.

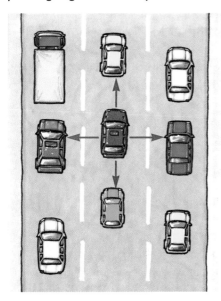

Figure 8: The red car is 'boxed in', giving the driver no escape if a problem happens ahead.

Look at Figures 10 and 11 below, and decide in each case which car you think is safest. Then read the explanation provided in the captions.

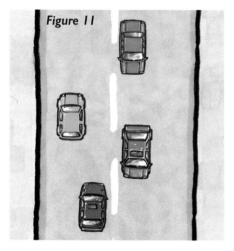

Figure 11

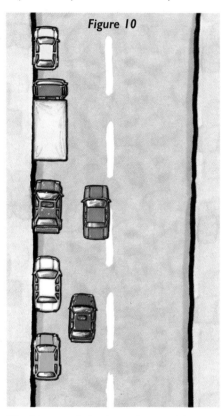

Figure 10

The green car is the only one in the middle of the lane – away from both the kerb and the oncoming traffic – and this is usually the ideal position. It allows the optimum 'space cushion' around your car – about a metre from the kerb – although if the road is too narrow for this, you will need to reduce your speed accordingly.

5. Be seen

It is vitally important when driving to make your intentions clear to everyone. You must get yourself noticed, or you increase the risk of having an accident. I am, of course, talking about signals. You must let both your position and your signals communicate to other road users – both motorists and pedestrians – what

The blue car is in the safest position because it is keeping its distance from the parked cars – about a metre or a car door's width away. This means that if a car pulls out or a door is opened, or worse if a child runs out in front of the lorry, there is space – and time – in which to react.

it is you intend doing next. And even when you've indicated your intentions to other drivers, still don't rely on them making the right move.

There are a number of ways to signal. You can indicate left or right with the indicators or with your arm, or you can use your positioning, your speed, horn, headlights, brake lights or your reverse lights. When you wish to change direction or change speed you need to look all around – including into your mirrors – and decide whether you need to signal, which signal to use and when it would be safe to give it.

Roundabouts seem to cause the most confusion as far as signals are concerned, so let's look at a couple of specific examples.

In the example below, driver A approaches the roundabout intending to turn left at the first exit but doesn't indicate. By A's positioning, driver B assumes he must be going straight ahead and taking the second exit, so B stops to give way to A. The whole point of a roundabout is to keep the traffic flowing smoothly, so that ideally cars can approach slowly and merge into a gap. If driver B has to stop

A's exit

because driver A didn't make his intentions clear, this may cause frayed tempers and an unnecessary tailback behind.

In the second example, above, driver A is turning right with the intention of taking the next exit marked, but he hasn't changed his position or his signal to the left. To driver B, this looks as if A is carrying on round to the next exit; B may well think it is safe to emerge and turn left at the first exit in which case they will collide. Driver C assumes that A is coming round and will wait, thus

holding up the traffic behind.

So as I hope you can see, clear communication with other traffic is essential. We need to indicate our intentions to others, just as we need them to let us know what they are doing or planning to do. Too many crashes – particularly at junctions or when cars are overtaking – are followed by cries of 'I didn't see him...' or 'I didn't believe he would pull out...'

So it is dangerous to assume another driver or pedestrian has seen you, or that they will understand from your signal what you intend doing.

Example Theory Test Questions

1. Drinking alcohol affects driving. Three likely effects of this are:

Mark three answers
- ○ a. faster reactions
- ☑ b. reduced co-ordination
- ○ c. improved concentration
- ☑ d. poor judgement
- ○ e. colour blindness
- ☑ f. increased confidence

2. You need to wear glasses or contact lenses in order to meet the minimum legal eyesight requirements for driving. You should wear them when driving:

Mark one answer
- ☑ a. at all times
- ○ b. at night only
- ○ c. in poor visibility only
- ○ d. only when you feel it is necessary

3. In an emergency your reaction time can be affected by the:

Mark one answer
- ○ a. weather conditions
- ○ b. road conditions
- ☑ c. state of your health
- ○ d. speed of your car

4. The law states that to drive a motor vehicle, you must be able to read a car number plate, 79.4mm (3.1 inches) high, from a distance of:

Mark one answer
- ○ a. 75 feet (23 metres)
- ☑ b. 67 feet (20.5 metres)
- ○ c. 90 feet (27.5 metres)
- ○ d. 100 feet (30.5 metres)

5. When driving for long distances on a motorway, you may feel tired. The *Highway Code* advises that in these circumstances you should:

Mark one answer
- ○ a. pull up on the hard shoulder and rest at reasonably frequent intervals
- ○ b. turn on the radio, as it could help concentration
- ☑ c. ensure your vehicle is well ventilated, and when necessary stop at a service area and walk around
- ○ d. increase speed to reduce your journey time

6. You are being overtaken and you see oncoming traffic close ahead. You should:

Mark one answer

- a. reduce speed so that the overtaking vehicle may move in ahead of you
- b. increase speed so that the overtaking vehicle may move in behind you
- c. reduce speed and flash your headlights so that the overtaking driver knows it is safe to move in ahead of you
- d. increase speed, and sound your horn to warn all the road users

7. You are travelling in a stream of traffic. You check your mirrors and realise that the car behind is very close to you. You should:

Mark one answer

- a. increase speed to widen the gap behind
- b. decrease speed to leave a bigger gap ahead
- c. maintain a steady speed and gap
- d. tap your brake pedal continuously to flash your brake lights

8. You are travelling on a dry road, in a well-maintained vehicle, at 60mph. You are alert and need to brake in an emergency. You are unable to stop in less than:

Mark one answer

- a. 73 metres (240 feet)
- b. 76 metres (250 feet)
- c. 85 metres (280 feet)
- d. 96 metres (315 feet)

9. Your medical condition forces you to take drugs that might affect your driving. You should consult:

Mark one answer

- a. DVLA Swansea
- b. Driving Standards Agency
- c. the police
- d. your doctor

10. You are approaching an oncoming vehicle. Both you and the other vehicle are travelling at 55mph. The gap between you is closing at :

Mark one answer

- a. 110mph
- b. 82.5mph
- c. 56mph
- d. 220mph

11. You are driving along and you double the speed of your vehicle. In doing so, your braking distance in an emergency will:

Mark one answer

○ a. remain constant

○ b. double

○ c. treble

✓ d. quadruple

12. You are waiting to turn left from a minor to a major road. You see a car approaching fast from the right, which is signalling left. You should:

Mark one answer

○ a. anticipate the signal and start to emerge

○ b. select neutral and apply the handbrake

✓ c. wait long enough to be sure the vehicle is turning left

○ d. emerge quickly in case of problems

13. It is raining and you are following a vehicle ahead. You should leave a minimum time gap of:

Mark one answer

○ a. 1 second

○ b. 2 seconds

○ c. 3 seconds

✓ d. 4 seconds

14. You intend to turn left from a major road onto a side road. Some people are already crossing the road into which you wish to turn. You should:

Mark one answer

○ a. wave to signal them to continue crossing

✓ b. slow down, stop if necessary and allow them to cross

○ c. sound your horn to warn them of your presence

○ d. drive on as you have the right of way

15. The term 'thinking distance' refers to:

Mark one answer

✓ a. the distance travelled from the moment a hazard is seen, to the time the brakes are applied

○ b. the distance that a driver thinks it will take him to stop

○ c. a distance of one metre for each mph of speed from the car in front

○ d. a distance of 1½ times the speed you are travelling

16. You are travelling at 70mph. Every second your car will cover a distance expressed in feet of approximately:

Mark one answer
- ○ a. 70 feet
- ○ b. 95 feet
- ○ c. 105 feet
- ○ d. 140 feet

17. Drinking and driving can cause three of the following:

Mark three answers
- ○ a. less control
- ○ b. increased awareness of hazards
- ○ c. quicker reactions
- ○ d. false sense of confidence
- ○ e. poor judgement of speed

18. You are an alert driver, travelling along a motorway in dry conditions in a well-maintained vehicle; you should keep a minimum distance from the vehicle in front, for each mph of your speed, of:

Mark one answer
- ○ a. 3 yards/metres
- ○ b. 2 yards/metres
- ○ c. 1 yard/metre
- ○ d. 0.5 yard/metre

19. You must not drive if the proportion of alcohol in each 100 millilitres of your breath exceeds:

Mark one answer
- ○ a. 35 microgrammes
- ○ b. 50 microgrammes
- ○ c. 80 microgrammes
- ○ d. 107 microgrammes

20. You intend to park on the left, just beyond a junction on the left. You should indicate your intentions:

Mark one answer
- ○ a. 20 metres before the junction
- ○ b. just before the junction
- ○ c. just as you pass the junction
- ○ d. well before the junction

21. You see people waiting at a zebra crossing. No one has stepped on to the crossing. You:

Mark one answer
- ○ a. must give a slowing down arm signal and stop
- ○ b. may drive across with care
- ○ c. must sound your horn
- ○ d. must stop

22. You have waited at a level crossing where the half barriers have been down for over three minutes but no train has come. You should:

Mark one answer

- ✓ a. phone the signalman for advice
- ○ b. carefully drive round the barriers and proceed
- ○ c. try to lift the barrier manually
- ○ d. wait another three minutes and then telephone the signalman for advice

23. You are on a dual carriageway. You wish to overtake, but check your mirror and see that the car behind has changed lanes to overtake you. You should:

Mark one answer

- ○ a. tap the foot brake to show your brake lights
- ✓ b. not signal or change position until the car has overtaken you
- ○ c. signal and pull out as rapidly as possible to overtake
- ○ d. signal to tell the driver behind that you wish to overtake

24. When driving in fog at night and travelling at a safe speed, you are dazzled by another vehicle following too close behind. You should:

Mark one answer

- ○ a. increase speed
- ✓ b. decrease speed and temporarily turn the mirror away to avoid dazzle
- ○ c. apply your rear fog lights
- ○ d. stay at the same speed and try to reduce the effects of the dazzle

25. You are normally only allowed to overtake on the right. In three of the situations below you may overtake on the left:

Mark three answers

- ✓ a. in queues of slow-moving traffic when traffic in the lane to your right is moving more slowly
- ○ b. on a two-lane dual carriageway
- ○ c. when nearing a motorway exit road where you will exit
- ✓ d. where the vehicle in front is signalling right
- ✓ e. in a one-way street

26. You should use your horn:

Mark one answer

- ✓ a. to alert other road users to your presence
- ○ b. to acknowledge other road users
- ○ c. to signal your irritation to other road users
- ○ d. to signal to other road users that they have made a mistake

27. You must never reverse your vehicle:

Mark one answer

- ○ a. near a lamp post
- ✓ b. for longer than is necessary
- ○ c. from a major to a minor road
- ○ d. into your driveway

28. If you were blind in one eye you would be able to drive:

Mark one answer

- ○ a. a lightweight car only
- ✓ b. any mechanically propelled vehicle for which you are qualified
- ○ c. no vehicle at all
- ○ d. a motorcycle only

29. If you have tunnel vision it means:

Mark one answer

- ✓ a. a narrow field of vision directly ahead
- ○ b. difficulty in focusing directly ahead
- ○ c. excellent vision in the dark
- ○ d. exceptional long distance vision

30. After leaving a motorway your perception of speed is likely to make you feel that you are travelling:

Mark one answer

- ○ a. faster than you really are
- ✓ b. slower than you really are
- ○ c. much faster than you really are
- ○ d. at about your true speed

Answers and Explanations

1. b., d. and f. are correct and often produce a lethal combination.
2. a.
3. c. is correct. You see a danger and you act. The time between seeing and acting is called your reaction time – the time it takes you to think – and can be affected by the state of your health. You should not confuse this with the fact that how far your car will travel during this time (thinking distance) will depend on its speed. Let's suppose you are travelling at 30mph. You see a danger and it then takes you one second to remove your foot from the accelerator (about ¾ of a second is normal). During this time you would travel 45 feet. At 70mph you would travel 105 feet.
4. b.
5. c.
6. a. is correct. You have no safe choice but to reduce speed. 'b' would be particularly dangerous if the overtaking driver also did the same. 'c' is not practical as the overtaking driver probably could not see your headlights anyway.
7. b. is correct. This is the safest option. More space ahead will allow you to brake less harshly if there is a problem, reducing the chance of the car behind hitting you.
8. a.
9. d.
10. a. is correct. Adding the two speeds together gives the answer.
11. d. is correct. If you double your speed you quadruple your braking distance.
12. c. Don't assume you know what the signal means. Be sure.
13. d.
14. b. is correct. The pedestrians have priority if they are already crossing.
15. a.
16. c. is correct. Your speed plus half your speed gives you the answer in feet. 70 + 35 = 105.
17. a., d. and e.
18. c.
19. a.
20. c.
21. b.
22. a.
23. b. is correct. Anything else causes danger or confusion.
24. b.
25. a., d. and e.
26. a. is correct. Don't use your horn in anger, but don't be afraid to use it when it may help.
27. b.
28. b.
29. a.
30. b.

2. Sharing the Road

Risk Taking and Accident Statistics

Life is full of risks and most of the time we can choose whether to take or avoid them. Generally we take risks because we believe that we will gain more than we might lose. For example, you might choose not to climb a mountain because you wish to avoid the risk of getting stuck or lost up it, but you could take the risk because the perceived benefit – fame, excitement, whatever – is far greater.

These days we understand much better the risks involved in driving. We understand far more how accidents are caused and who has them and we know that accidents have more to do with the driver's attitudes and beliefs than with physical skill.

But we still take the risk of driving excessively fast, for example, because we believe it will get us to our destination quicker. Most of the time we don't arrive any quicker; sometimes we don't arrive at all – and yet, despite recognising that speed can kill, we still choose to drive too fast. As drivers, we choose to take risks where we really have very little, if anything at all, to gain.

Perhaps the reason we choose to take so many risks is because we are unaware of the facts. So I shall now introduce you to a few statistics.

Accident statistics

Considering how skilful and safe we think we are behind the wheel, we manage to smash up our cars with alarming frequency. The number of accidents involving a car insurance claim continues to rise and was last estimated at 3,200,000 every year, which equates to six accidents every minute. Few of us believe we are likely to cause an accident; we assume that accidents only happen to

other people, and in any case are always the fault of the other driver.

There is no escaping the fact that people cause accidents. In fact, 95 per cent of all accidents involve an element of human error. The latest figures available (illustrated below) show that in Great Britain we collide with each other at an alarming rate and often with tragic consequences.

The number of deaths and serious injuries has gone down over the last few years, which is excellent. The number of slight injuries has, however, unfortunately gone up.

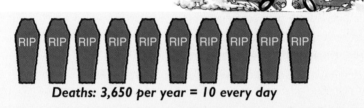

Deaths: 3,650 per year = 10 every day

Serious injury: 46,531 per year = 127 every day

Slight injury: 265,008 per year = 726 every day

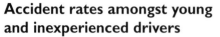

Accident rates amongst young and inexperienced drivers

Road accidents are the major killer of young people between the ages of 5 and 34 and the cause of one third of deaths amongst young men aged between 15 and 24. In fact people who die in road accidents are, on average, 25 years younger than those dying from all other major causes.

Statistics show that young and new drivers hold only 10 per cent of licenses but are involved in 20 per cent of road accidents in which someone is injured.

Where do accidents happen?

Road accidents account for 95 per cent of all transport deaths – 50 times more than deaths from rail accidents and 70 times more than deaths from air or sea travel. It is therefore interesting to note where most of these road accidents actually occur.

Towns

The majority of road accidents actually occur in towns. Of all accidents that take place anywhere, those in towns account for:

- 70 per cent involving injury
- 95 per cent involving pedestrians
- 90 per cent involving pedal cyclists
- 57 per cent involving car occupants.

In fact, 80 per cent of all accident injuries involving child pedestrians occur on minor roads in towns.

Rural areas

While there are fewer accidents in rural areas they tend to be more severe than those occurring in towns. Some 60 per cent of them take place on A-roads and it therefore may not

surprise you that 75 per cent of people injured are actually car occupants.

Motorways

Despite the terrible descriptions of motorway accidents that you hear on the news, motorways are in fact the safest of all our roads. However, because of the speed and volume of traffic, motorway accidents can often result in serious injury or death. Indeed motorway accidents account for some 10 per cent of all injuries outside urban areas.

What are people doing when they have accidents?

- 3% Left turn
- 1.0% U-turn
- 0.5% Reversing
- 48% Going ahead
- 15% Rounding bend
- 4% Overtaking
- 15% Right turn
- 13.5% Other

Common Accident Scenarios

This short section of this book will, I hope, help you learn not just the answers to the Theory Test questions, but also how to put them into practice.

Your sole objective in studying this book, learning to drive and passing your Theory and Practical Test should be that you finish up as a qualified driver who will be accident free. Almost every driving syllabus, from beginner to advanced, discusses the need to understand why road accidents happen so that we can identify the risk factors early and prevent accidents occurring.

On the pages that follow, I have set out ten of the most common accident scenarios. Each scenario contains a description of what tends to happen and why, identifies the risk indicators from the start, and gives suggestions for ways to reduce risks and avoid crashing. Research has demonstrated that the better your perception of risk, the more time you will have to prevent or avoid an accident. My aim in this section is to improve your perception.

1. 'What difference does 5mph Make?'

When we say 'speed kills' most people imagine someone driving at 100mph on a motorway. In reality, just 5mph too fast in the wrong situation is a more common killer, particularly if a pedestrian is involved in the accident.

Earlier on, discussing reaction times, I explained that your car keeps moving during the time it takes you to come off the gas and start to brake. The greater your speed, the further your car will travel before the brakes start to slow it down. We tend to believe that most speed is lost when we start braking. In fact most speed is lost in the period just before we stop, if we haven't already hit something.

Figure 1 shows what happens when a pedestrian walks out in front of a car travelling at 30mph. If the driver hits the brakes when the pedestrian is still at least 14 metres away (about 45 feet), there would be enough space in which to stop.

Figure 2 shows the same scenario, but this time with the car travelling at 35mph. If the driver hits the brakes at the same point, the car will still be doing 18mph when it hits the pedestrian.

Outcome: Depending on the impact, the pedestrian will be thrown onto the bonnet, windscreen or roof of the car and either killed or seriously injured. Damage to the car is likely to mean it needs towing away.

Suggestion: Reducing the risk is mostly a matter of backing off the power especially when it is likely that there will be pedestrians around.

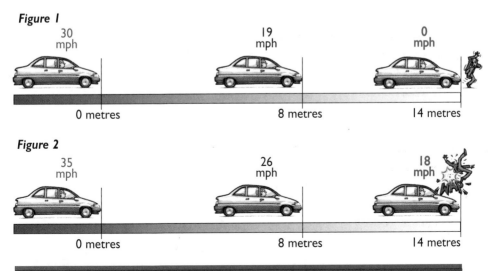

Figure 1

| 30 mph | 19 mph | 0 mph |
| 0 metres | 8 metres | 14 metres |

Figure 2

| 35 mph | 26 mph | 18 mph |
| 0 metres | 8 metres | 14 metres |

2. The 'pull out'

The most common accident in towns is caused by drivers failing to stop at a Stop or Give Way line, whether it is through tiredness, impatience, distraction or because they have misjudged the distance and speed of approaching vehicles.

If you are the one driving along the main road, pay particular attention to traffic in the side roads, because it could pull out straight in front of you.

In Figure 3, the parked car is a perennial problem. The driver in the side road cannot see the car on the main road and vice versa.

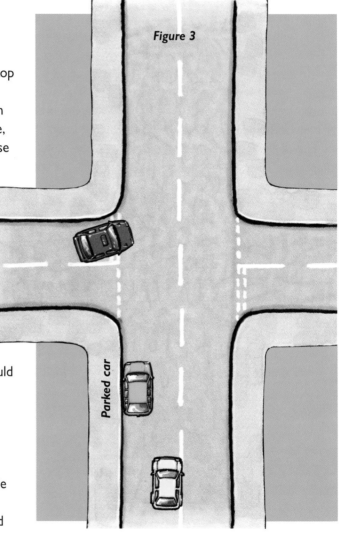

Figure 3

Parked car

Suggestion: Give the parked car a wide berth so that you can both see and be seen, and back off the power a little, just in case.

And remember, of course, that leaving your car where the blue car is parked is both inconsiderate and dangerous.

3. Turning at junctions

If it were somehow possible to do away with all our road junctions, there would be a very dramatic fall in the accident rate. The basic trouble with junctions is that there are too many people trying to achieve too many different things.

When you turn off at junctions (Figure 4), all manner of things can go wrong. There may be a motorist right on your tail, a motorcyclist filtering through the traffic on one side or the other, or a pedestrian waiting to cross the road you are turning into. What if the driver behind assumes you won't stop, but the pedestrian steps out into the road to cross. If there is a cyclist approaching the turning, is it safe to turn in front of the bike?

Suggestion: Unless a turn-off is completely straightforward, slow down even more than usual. This may be frustrating for you and for the driver behind, but it reduces the risk of collision should you decide to wait on account of the pedestrian or the cyclist.

When turning right (Figure 5), approaching traffic is an additional risk. Resist the urge to turn just because you are holding up traffic behind or because the car in front of you is turning.

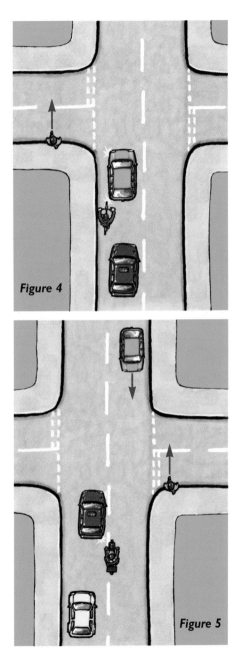

Figure 4

Figure 5

4. Overtaking (side road)

If overtaking involves driving on the 'wrong side of the road', you need to be absolutely certain the road will remain clear, and junctions are obviously a problem. It is not for nothing that the *Highway Code* advises you not to overtake near junctions.

Overtaking at a junction means relying on no driver coming out of the side road while you are passing, and Figure 6 shows what is likely to happen if someone does pull out.

When coming out of a side road, it is only too easy to think: 'If it's clear to the right, I'll go straight out.' We may not look to the left until it's too late and we are already halfway out.

As I explained earlier, you must look both ways before emerging from a junction and you should be looking left as you move to the left.

Never assume that a driver in a side road can see you overtaking, and will wait for you to pass.

Outcome: A possible head-on collision which, depending on the impact, might cause a further collision with the (green) car being overtaken.

Suggestion: Don't overtake at or near a side road. Before pulling out of a junction yourself, remember to check to the left.

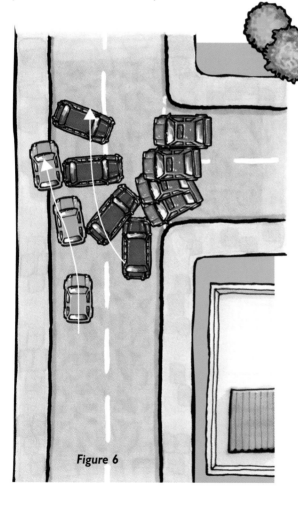

Figure 6

5. Single-vehicle crash

Young male drivers tend to have more accidents of this type than the rest of the population, particularly on country roads. It is generally caused by a failure to slow down for what appears to be a harmless bend.

Figure 7

We may believe our car really will corner 'as if on rails', but unfortunately grip is mostly dependent on tyres and road surface, and cannot work if you enter a bend too fast.

Figure 7 shows what can happen if a typical bend on a narrow road is taken at too high a speed. At first the back of the car will slide away, little by little, then the car goes into a spin, often only stopping when it hits a tree, or some other immovable object.

Outcome: On a right-hand bend, the passenger may be killed as a result of the collision with a stationary object.

Suggestion: Once you've lost control, it may be difficult, if not impossible, to regain it. Avoid getting into this situation in the first place by making sure you slow down enough for bends.

Should you encounter a near miss when cornering, rather than blaming the road, the wet, or the black ice, try and learn from the experience.

6. Too close for comfort

■ Pedestrians

At some times in our lives, we have all taken a step into the road, then looked to see if there is any traffic coming.

Figure 8 shows pedestrians on the pavement, though they may of course not stay there. When driving past pedestrians like this, it is much safer to assume that they are young children, old-age pensioners, deaf or even drunk, and likely to step into the road at any moment.

Suggestion: Move further into the middle of the road and give the pedestrians room to get it wrong and not get hurt.

■ Cyclists

If you are a cyclist yourself, you'll know exactly what it feels like when a car flashes past your handlebars at 40mph and more. In Figure 9, the resulting slipstream, not to mention the shock, may well cause a cyclist to move further out from the kerb and into the path of following traffic.

Suggestion: Give cyclists plenty of room. If you are unable to move out across the centre line, then hold back until it is possible. Squeezing through at 40mph is too dangerous.

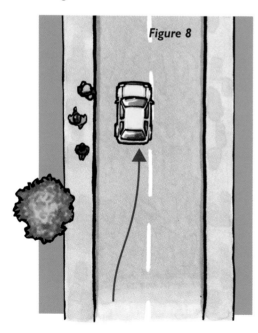

Figure 8

Figure 9

■ Parked Cars

Since we cannot remove the problem that parked cars represent, we must learn to live with it. At sometime or other, we have all stepped out from between parked cars – as in Figure 10 – in order to cross the road, but when children do this they are very hard to spot. Drivers, moreover, often find it difficult getting into, and out of, their cars because of the close proximity of other traffic. Remember that a door when thrown open produces a 'wall of steel' a metre wide.

Suggestion: Keep well clear of parked cars just in case a pedestrian walks out or a door is thrown open; and if you can't keep clear, slow down. You may have to stop suddenly.

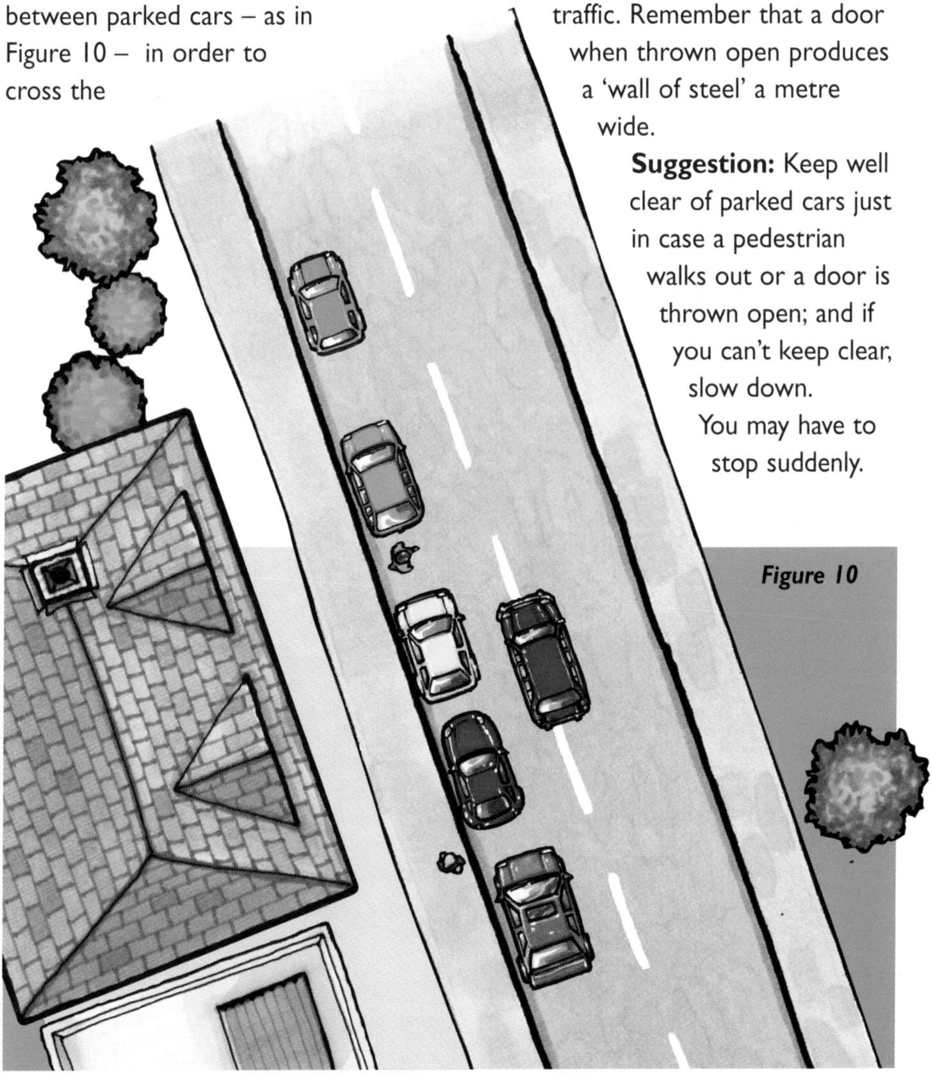

Figure 10

7. Overtaking (country road)

Overtaking always contains an element of risk, which is why you need to take special care. There are clearly more dangers overtaking on a two-way country road than on a dual carriageway, if only because traffic may be coming in the other direction and you will have to drive on the 'wrong' side of the road when passing.

It is easy to misjudge the speed and distance of approaching traffic and where overtaking is concerned this lack of judgement could be fatal.

The gap between you and oncoming traffic can disappear alarmingly quickly. Remember that if you are driving at 60mph (the national speed limit on a two-way road) and oncoming traffic is also doing 60mph, the gap between you is closing at 120mph. This means that the gap shortens about 60 metres (180 feet) every second.

Figure 11 depicts an all too common sight for drivers using country roads. A long, straight stretch of road with fields on either side can affect your judgement.

The type of impact shown may cause one or both of the cars to leave the road and possibly hit a tree.

Outcome: Although the driver may survive the first smash, the second impact with the tree might be fatal.

Suggestion: Ask yourself whether you can really judge the other driver's speed accurately enough to overtake? If in doubt, don't pass.

Figure 11

Figure 12: are you sure that you can see everything ahead of the car in front?

8. Tail-gating

Driving up the exhaust pipe of a vehicle in front of you is never advisable, even when you think you can see past it, as in Figure 12.

Where do we get the idea that other drivers are predictable?

You may think you can follow behind a car closely and safely because you can see past it. Britain is a country of animal lovers and, though common sense may dictate otherwise, many people will automatically stamp on the brake to avoid a stray cat or dog.

Following blindly – as shown in Figure 13 – is dangerous. A driver in this situation has no idea at all what is happening

up ahead. The lorry driver may hit a stationary vehicle, in which case the driver behind – expecting to see brake lights, which now won't appear – will hit the lorry.

Suggestion: Either drop back or, if the road is clear, overtake.

Figure 13: this close behind a lorry you're blind.

9. Communication

Earlier in the book, I discussed the need to 'be seen' when driving and how to use signals to communicate your intentions to other drivers. I used a couple of examples at a roundabout to make my point. The problem of course is that not everyone drives by the rules, and you can never be sure that a signal is being correctly given.

Figure 14 shows a driver on a roundabout indicating left, yet the position of the car isn't what you would expect. It is too close to the island in the middle of the roundabout, leading one to suppose that the driver is planning to take an exit further round the roundabout.

Suggestion: Keep a very close eye on other drivers and leave them plenty of room. But most importantly, don't just rely on signals. Look for other evidence – such as the driver's speed and position – to confirm your impression. If you are not exactly sure what the driver is planning to do at the roundabout, move out slowly and, as you do, keep on checking carefully.

Figure 14

10. Relying on others not making a wrong move

We all make mistakes when we drive, and we should never rely on others not making a wrong move. In Figure 15, the pedestrian crossing the road may only cross to the middle and wait for you to pass, but what if they judge your speed badly. How many times have you run across the road in front of a car, forcing the driver to brake? We are all capable of doing daft things at times, but please do remember that people damage much more easily than cars and are much harder to repair.

Suggestion: Slow down and, if possible, move further towards the kerb (away from the pedestrian). If necessary, stop and let the pedestrian cross. Tapping your horn may help, but not all pedestrians will hear you.

Figure 15

Imagine an Accident

It is all too easy to fall into the trap of believing that accidents only happen to other people. Imagining yourself in an accident is not easy, but imagining yourself as the cause of a serious accident is just as distressing. Still, it is a worthwhile exercise to try if it makes you more aware of the risks around you and keeps you safer.

Using your imagination also helps when it comes to predicting the possible outcome of a situation as well as the behaviour of other drivers. The ability to ask yourself 'what if...?' or 'what might happen next?' is fundamental to your safety when driving, and the next few pages should help you explore this a little.

Now look at the following four accident scenarios. In each case, a short explanation and a diagram shows a situation that resulted, just seconds later, in a serious accident. All are real accidents that have actually happened.

Take a look at each diagram and, using your imagination, try and work out what happened next and who or what was hurt. You may also want to apportion blame and decide who was

responsible. When you have decided on your own version, turn to the next pages to find out what actually happened.

Scenario 1

Although no vehicle is travelling at more than 30mph, the van has faulty brakes.

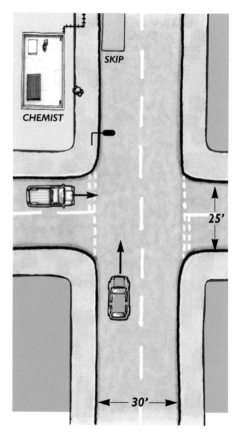

Scenario 2 (right)

The cars in the left-hand side road are parked. No vehicle is travelling at more than 30mph.

Scenario 3 (bottom right)

The car, travelling at 60mph, sees the lorry signal and moves to the right-hand lane.

Scenario 4 (left)

On this dual carriageway the two cars at the bottom of the picture are both travelling at 60mph. Ahead in the left-hand lane is a yellow car and, following very close behind it, an ambulance carrying elderly people.

Accidents – what actually happened

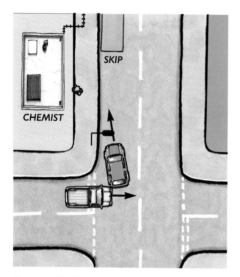

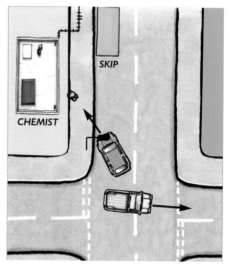

Scenario 1 – crossroads 1

A van with faulty brakes overshoots the Give Way lines, crashing into the nearside rear of the car. Although neither vehicle is doing more than 30mph, the collision causes the car to change direction.

Veering between a lamp post and a skip, it mounts the pavement, killing a pedestrian standing outside the chemist's shop. The car then hits the chemist's shop before it is brought to a stop by the railings.

In this actual accident, the van driver then absconded. The case went to the Coroner's Court only, where the car driver was found innocent of any wrongdoing.

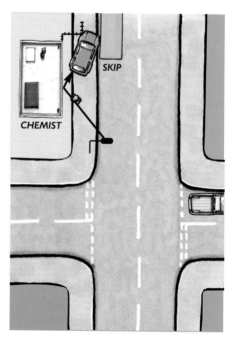

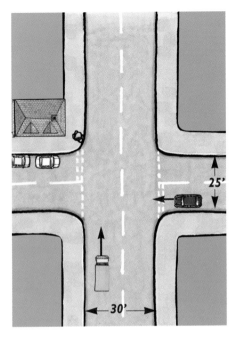

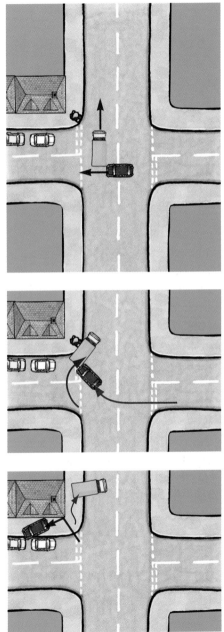

Scenario 2 – crossroads 2

A sales rep driving the blue car comes straight out from a side road with Give Way lines (he claimed the road was icy). He hits the offside rear of a van travelling along the main road – both vehicles doing 30mph – causing the van to spin round and onto the pavement. A pedestrian waiting for a lift to work is hit by the nearside rear of the van and is killed. The blue car careers into the side road opposite where it mounts the pavement, hitting a house and two parked cars.

In this second real accident the rep was found guilty of reckless driving.

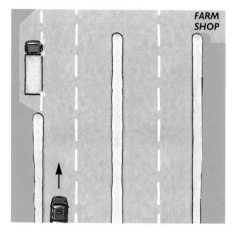

FARM SHOP

FARM SHOP

Scenario 3 – ambiguous signal

A driver on a stretch of dual carriageway is well in front of the main stream of traffic but still within the 60mph speed limit. Seeing that a lorry driver parked in a lay-by is signalling right, the car driver moves into the right-hand lane without loss of speed. But the lorry driver – delivering supplies to a farm shop on the opposite side of the road – turns across the whole width of the carriageway and into a gap in the central strip. The driver of the car reacts, steers to the left and brakes hard, locking up the wheels. The collision takes the roof off the car as it is caught by the rear of the trailer, and the driver is killed.

In this case the lorry driver was convicted of driving without due care and attention.

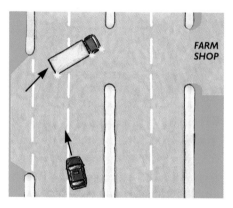

FARM SHOP

FARM SHOP

Scenario 4 – racing

Two drivers – one in a blue car, the other in a brown car – are racing each other along a dual carriageway. Ahead of them in the left-hand lane is a yellow car, closely followed by an ambulance ferrying elderly people. At the last moment, the driver of the yellow car signals to turn into a side road on the left, and the ambulance driver has to swerve into the right-hand lane to avoid a collision.

The two drivers coming up behind have already slowed slightly – according to witnesses later – and when they begin to brake are doing no more than 60mph. The blue car driver decides to pass the ambulance on the left but, still doing 25mph or so, hits the slowed and turning yellow car hidden behind it, which spins round and hits a lamp post on the other side of the junction. The brown car, in turn, hits the ambulance which crashes through the central barrier and onto the opposite carriageway, causing minor impacts with two other vehicles. Several elderly people in the ambulance receive injuries, though the drivers are unhurt.

Evidence was later given that the drivers of the blue and brown cars were racing one another, but this case never made it to court as too many were to blame.

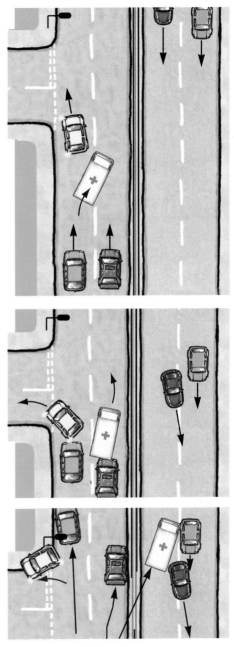

Risk Factors

I want to talk to you about how to minimise the risks you are exposed to when driving and will do so by dividing this section into three areas:

- Risk factors associated with different road conditions
- Risk factors associated with different types of vehicle
- Risk factors associated with vulnerable road users.

1. Risk factors associated with different road conditions

First of all, it is vitally important that your car is well maintained so that it can stand up to the road and weather conditions. It is the driver's responsibility to make sure the car is checked and serviced regularly.

Tyres: check them daily for any obvious signs of wear and tear, and check their pressures once a week. If you are setting out on a long journey or you know your car will be especially heavily laden with passengers or baggage, check your tyres before you start out.

Brakes: make sure they're working efficiently by regularly trying them out at the start of a journey.

Other items: check the oil, water and fuel levels regularly, and ensure the windows, windscreen, lights and mirrors are all clean and free from smears, dust and grease. Check that the windscreen wipers are working properly and the washer bottle is topped up.

It is also important that you know how to work the de-misters and the ventilation system to prevent your car from misting up. In heavy rain the windscreen can mist up very rapidly, and you will need to keep warm air blowing on it.

The key to handling your own car, when dealing with changing weather and road conditions and with the various times of day, is your speed. In the first section I discussed separation distances, and the need to leave enough room between you and the vehicle in front. Now I want to look again at the first part of rule 57 in the *Highway Code*:

Drive at a speed that will allow you to stop well within the distance you can see to be clear.

This means you must plan your speed according to visibility. The further ahead you can see clearly, the faster you can drive. If something

In heavy rain you will need to keep warm air blowing on the windscreen.

unexpected happens on the road ahead, you have to be able to stop safely. Where you are unable to see the road ahead – because there is the brow of a hill, say – then you need to use your imagination to anticipate what may be hurtling towards you and you should slow down.

Each time you start your car or turn off from one road into another, you need to decide on a safe speed for the conditions so that you can stop safely within the distance you can see to be clear.

Rain

When driving on wet roads, remember that if you have to brake suddenly it will take you at least twice as long to stop the car. Tyres do not grip the surface of the road well when it is wet and the risk of the wheels locking up is far greater. To keep the tyres gripping, you should apply less pressure to the brakes than you would normally do on a dry road surface. This means driving slower in the first

place, especially when there are pedestrians or children around.

Use dipped headlights in the rain to help you see and to let others know that you are there. And remember to ensure your windscreen is clear and the washer bottle is full. Often, with a few drops of rain, the wipers just smear the windscreen and you will need to clear it from the washer bottle.

If you have to drive through flood water or a ford, choose the point that appears to be the shallowest. Drive slowly in first gear, slipping the clutch and keeping the engine speed high and steady so that you don't stall. If you go too fast you risk making waves which could flood the engine and cause it to cut out. Once through the water, test your brakes by driving slowly with your right foot on the accelerator and your left foot pressing lightly on the brake.

Fog

Driving in fog puts you under extreme pressure because you have to concentrate so hard. The worrying thing about fog is that it can come down so suddenly, like a blanket. However, it can also be patchy, which is all the more disconcerting because in the clear stretches some drivers pick up speed again, only to find themselves heading straight for another patch even denser than the last. Accidents in fog are usually multiple pile-ups and often there are casualties.

It is essential that you make allowances for driving in fog. If you come across it unexpectedly and have an appointment to keep, just accept that you will be late and don't push yourself to drive too fast. If possible, turn back.

If you really must drive, use your dipped headlights and high-intensity rear fog lights if visibility is less than 100 metres. As the fog varies, remember to change your lights. It is an offence to use high-intensity rear fog lights if visibility is not less than 100 metres. If you are in a queue of traffic, and have been seen by traffic behind, it can be helpful to switch off your fog lights temporarily to avoid dazzling other drivers.

When you are following another vehicle in fog, leave plenty of room to stop. It can be very disorientating attempting to judge speed and distance when you are driving in a blur. It is also difficult to react quickly to the driver in front braking as the brake lights seem no brighter than any other lights. If you are hanging onto the lights of the vehicle in front, then you are driving much too close. Take extra care if you want to overtake in fog; visibility ahead can turn out to be far worse than you

When following another vehicle in fog, leave plenty of room to stop.

If you're starting off in deep snow, racing the engine will only dig you in.

originally thought and you won't see oncoming traffic in time.

At junctions – particularly emerging to the right – use your ears as well as your eyes. If you wind down the window, you can listen for any approaching traffic. While waiting to emerge, if you keep your foot on the brake pedal, your lights will warn any vehicles coming from behind that you are there. And, of course, never park anywhere that will put other drivers at risk because they can't see you soon enough.

Snow and ice

The main problem with falling snow is reduced visibility. Use your dipped headlights and be prepared to clear the front and rear windscreens and the lights by hand if snow is packing

onto them. While driving, increase the gap between you and the vehicle in front and test your brakes gently – packed snow around the wheels and brake linkages can affect your steering and braking.

If you have to brake on snow and ice your overall stopping distance can be at least 10 times as much as on a good road surface, because there is virtually no grip between your wheels and the road surface. All but the most gentle form of braking can lock the wheels, so you need to use your gears to hold back the speed of the car. Use very gentle brake pressure early to slow the car down and change into a lower gear sooner than normal. Avoid braking on a bend. Aim to get your speed right – by making maximum use of engine braking – before you get

On unlit roads you have no way of knowing what is ahead of you, beyond the range of your headlights.

into the bend and be gentle with the accelerator and the steering. Please note that if your front wheels lock you will be unable to steer, exposing you to the risk of an accident.

If you are starting off in deep snow, the wheels will dig in further if you race the engine. Use the highest gear you can and try to move the car backwards and forwards to get out of the rut.

Sunshine

The sun, especially when it is low in the sky, can affect your ability to concentrate and make it difficult to see properly. Wear sunglasses or put down the visor to reduce the glare, and avoid looking directly into the sun. Wet roads may also cause reflected glare, and in this case too you should slow down.

The time of day

Between dusk and dawn you will need to use your dipped headlights to increase your visibility. You must be able to stop within the range of your headlights or, if the road is lit and you can see further than the beam of your lights, within the distance you can see to be clear. On an unlit road you have no way of knowing what might be ahead of you, outside the range of your headlights, so slow down.

Skids

But what if, despite all the care you have taken, you suddenly lose control and get into a skid? First of all, try not to panic. To regain control of the car you will need to take your feet off all the pedals. Your instinct may well be to press down hard on all the pedals you can find, but believe me this will only make matters worse.

Let's suppose that the initial cause of the skid was too much pressure on the brake pedal so that the wheels locked and the car started to slide. You will need to take your foot off the brake and steer into the direction of the skid. I will explain what this means.

When you brake, the weight of the car is thrown forwards. (Just as, if you're standing up in a bus and the bus brakes you will be thrown forwards.) Because all the weight is thrown to the front of the car, the rear becomes too light. The rear wheels then have difficulty gripping the road surface, and are inclined to lock. If the rear wheels lock and you fail to take your foot off the brake – allowing them to start turning and grip the road again – you may well feel the back of the car sliding. If it slides to the right, you must steer to the right.

If the car slides to the left, steer to the left. This is what is meant by 'steering into a skid'.

Harsh accelerating or abrupt steering may also cause a skid. Again, remove the cause of the skid by taking your foot off the accelerator.

Traffic calming

In many areas, measures have been taken to slow down the speed of the traffic. On the approach to roundabouts on dual carriageways, for instance, you may well see horizontal yellow lines which create the effect of making you feel you are coming up too fast and need to slow down.

In residential areas, especially large housing estates with a lot of through traffic, speed bumps – sometimes called sleeping policemen – force drivers to slow down.

In some residential areas, speed bumps are used to force drivers to slow down.

2. Risk factors associated with different types of vehicle

I now want to draw your attention to the risk factors associated with other traffic and what you need to do to maximise your safety. It is important to be aware of.the handling problems that lorry and bus drivers and motorbike riders come up against, and how these problems can affect you.

The long wheel base on large vehicles means that the course they have to take when manoeuvring is not always immediately obvious. I remember following a bus one day and, seeing it indicate left, assumed it was going to pull up at a bus stop. So I checked my mirrors and was just starting to pull out to the right when the bus in front also started to move out to the right. As there was a junction ahead on the right, I assumed that was where it was heading, although I did think it strange that the driver had given the wrong signal.

Nevertheless I checked my mirrors again and moved back to the left, ready to pass the bus on the left-hand side. However, the bus turned left into a bus depot I had failed to notice. It was a near miss that really shook me up when I considered what might have happened had I actually been alongside the bus as it turned.

Buses and lorries are inevitably going to pull out to the right before turning left, or take a confusing course at roundabouts, junctions and entrances, and you should be aware of this. If you hang back you will have more visibility and more chance of working out what the driver of a large vehicle is intending to do as a result of the signal given.

You need to consider the speed of a large vehicle, especially if it is heavily laden and you are overtaking on a hill. A lorry will lose speed climbing a hill and you may want to overtake it. But try to do so before the hill comes to an end, because once the road levels out, or falls away downhill, a lorry will pick up speed quickly because of its weight. This could cause problems if you are on a two-way road and something is coming towards you.

Also bear in mind that drivers of large vehicles hate slowing down unnecessarily, and that the knock-on effect of a lorry slowing down can cause miles of tailback. So don't hog the middle lane of the motorway if you have a safe opportunity to move back into the left and let a lorry past. It can be extremely intimidating when the driver of a vehicle six times the size of yours is bearing down on you, flashing his lights; just ease back into the left and let him come through.

I have often heard on the news that bridges are being closed to high-sided vehicles because of strong winds, and you probably have too. Do bear in mind that a sudden gust of wind can cause lorries and caravans to blow over. Remember, if overtaking a large vehicle, that the strong gust of wind you experience as you pass can cause you to swerve to the right. Also make allowances for strong crosswinds affecting motorcyclists as you overtake; they could swerve dangerously close to you.

In wet weather, large vehicles – especially when travelling at speed – throw up an incredible amount of spray, making visibility very poor. Make sure you leave a larger separation gap than usual and that you have adjusted your speed to suit the conditions.

Finally, a word about buses and the need to show them consideration. Bus drivers expect others to let them pull out. Rule 79 in the *Highway Code* says:

> *Give way to buses whenever you can do so safely, especially when they signal to pull away from bus stops.*

If several cars have already come past a bus ignoring the signal, the driver is possibly going to try to pull out straight in front of you. So look out for buses and, if they are signalling to move away from a bus stop, give way if it is safe to do so.

Remember that high-sided vehicles can be blown over in exposed and windy situations.

3. Risk factors associated with vulnerable road users

The level of risk that road users face depends on the particular situation. Let's imagine the following scenarios:

- You are approaching a zebra crossing ahead of you, and knowing it to be a risky situation you look very closely all around you. There is no one to be seen and, in this particular instance, there is virtually no risk.
- This time as you approach the crossing you are talking to a passenger in the car and not really paying attention. You do not know whether someone might want to use the crossing – or indeed is actually on it – so you are increasing the level of risk.
- Now let's imagine that something is obstructing your view of the crossing. This could be a car parked illegally on the zigzag lines or simply a queue of traffic on the other side of the road, making it impossible to see whether anyone is waiting to cross. The risk is far greater in this situation.

The risk can be reduced as long as you take appropriate action, usually slowing down. Even in the first scenario, where the crossing is clear, it would be wise to slow down in order to assure yourself that no one will suddenly appear.

You do have a choice when it comes to reducing the risk element both to yourself and to other road users, regardless of how anyone else is behaving. There is nothing to be gained from compounding somebody else's mistakes. So even if someone is illegally parked on the zigzag lines, blocking your view of the crossing, you can still take action to reduce the level of risk, providing you are paying attention.

So who are these vulnerable road users and what safety practices can we observe to keep both them and us from harm? They fall into two categories:

- Vehicle users
- Pedestrians.

Vehicle users

By vehicle users I mean new and older drivers, cyclists and motorcyclists.

A new driver is anyone with less than two years' driving experience. Research shows that you are statistically far more likely to have an accident within the first two years of passing your driving test than after this time. Studies investigating the behaviour of novice drivers show that inexperienced drivers tend to concentrate on the control skills involved in vehicle handling, rather than on hazard recognition and decision-making.

Statistics also show that this has nothing to do with age, but everything to do with inexperience. Drivers who dither around, brake at the last moment and change lanes suddenly are a danger because they are such an unknown quantity and they put other drivers at risk. Inexperience is often the cause of this sort of erratic behaviour.

What has been discovered is that inexperienced drivers have more accidents because they fail to look as far down the road as experienced drivers. New drivers often look in the wrong place for information and fail to anticipate distant hazards. They tend not to see lights change to red as early as an experienced driver, so they slam their brakes on at the last minute. Nor are they so quick to see a bus pull up in front of them and so they swerve out to avoid it. And sometimes they see things so late that it is

Allow cyclists as much room as possible when overtaking.

impossible to rectify the situation and they have an accident.

As a driver you need to make allowances for inexperienced drivers, even though you will obviously be one yourself initially. Consider that the driver in front of you, not displaying L-plates, might have passed their test only the day before.

Two-wheeled transport

Cyclists and motorcyclists are particularly vulnerable road users, mainly because we so often fail to see them. Car drivers are programmed to look out for cars and so anything of a lesser width is not registered. The campaign THINK ONCE. THINK TWICE. THINK BIKE was designed to help drivers overcome this problem.

Look out for cyclists at road

junctions especially, and try to allow them as much room as possible when overtaking. If you can't give them plenty of room, you need to slow down. Cyclists, particularly the young or those laden down with shopping and bulky objects, can wobble or swerve suddenly. Even professional-looking cyclists in cycling shorts and wearing helmets will not wish to risk damaging their wheels in potholes or drain covers, so be prepared for them to avoid poor road surfaces. And many cyclists may suddenly dismount if the hill they are climbing becomes too steep.

Try to anticipate the actions of a cyclist. A glance over the shoulder, for instance, could mean that they intend turning right and will move into your path. The same goes for a motorcyclist. And remember that they are all exposed to bad weather, slippery or uneven road surfaces and crosswinds.

The other day I was stuck in creeping traffic up to a roundabout a mile ahead. I was in the middle of three lanes, with a small van behind me. I soon became aware that the van was positioned well to the right of the lane, virtually over the lane markings. At first I thought this was just inconsiderate, as a motorcyclist

Even professional-looking cyclists in cycling shorts, wearing helmets and proud of their bikes, may avoid poor road surfaces so as to not damage their wheels, so be prepared for them to swerve unpredictably.

Motorcyclists are also exposed to bad weather, slippery or uneven road surfaces and crosswinds.

coming down between the middle and right-hand lanes could not get past. Then I noticed the driver grinning at his passenger and looking in his right-door mirror. He was deliberately positioned to block the passage of all the motorcyclists – and there were several – trying to get by. Perhaps he was relieving the boredom of queuing, but he was amusing himself and his passengers by creating an inconvenience for others. Motorcyclists have the same right to be on the road as you have, so it is important to make allowances and give them plenty of room.

Elderly drivers

When my grandfather was in his eighties, he asked me what I thought about elderly drivers and whether they should be barred from driving after a certain age.

I told him that I thought the problem with elderly drivers is that they are often over-cautious. Their reactions are not necessarily as good as they might have been in their younger days. Their eyesight may well be failing and, in spite of opticians' help, they simply cannot judge speed and distance as well as they once could. They perhaps tire more easily. They can get out of touch with changes to rules and regulations.

But can this be a yardstick by which to measure all older drivers? Are there no older drivers prepared to recognise their own limitations and drive safely? Of course there are. It is up to other road users to recognise an older driver and make allowances for them. Older drivers have years more experience than other motorists, and if they are driving slower than you they are nevertheless driving within their capabilities. That has to be better than a young, inexperienced person driving like a bolted horse with no thought or consideration for either his or anyone else's safety.

Pedestrians

All pedestrians should be seen as being vulnerable road users – particularly children, the elderly and disabled. It is dangerous to assume that every single pedestrian is physically and mentally fit enough not to step out and finish up under the wheels of a car.

Generally speaking, you should give way to pedestrians who are crossing the road as you turn into a junction. If they are still on the pavement as you turn into the road, make sure – before continuing – that they have seen you

and are not going to step out.

In particular, look out for elderly people crossing the road. Their hearing and eyesight might not be so good. They cannot necessarily judge the speed of traffic so well and don't always realise the dangers involved in crossing the road. Nor will they be able to move quickly if they have misjudged the gap, so be prepared to slow down and give them time to clear the road.

Disabled people need particular consideration. It is obviously difficult to tell if someone is deaf, but take care if someone fails to look your way as you get closer. There are guide dogs for the hard of hearing as well as for the blind. The guide dog for someone with hearing problems usually has an orange lead and collar. The guide dog for a visually disabled pedestrian has a loop type of harness. A white stick indicates the carrier is blind. If the stick has two reflective red bands around it, the pedestrian is also hard of hearing. Again, give these people plenty of time to cross the road.

As a driver, take great care when near children. Children can dash impulsively across the road simply because they have spotted friends on the other side. Children are especially unpredictable and you really need to

Be especially careful of children – they can dash impulsively across the road simply because they have spotted friends on the other side.

be driving slowly and with special care in residential areas, near schools, parks and near ice-cream vans. Be aware of the times of day when children are going to and from schools. If there is a school-crossing warden holding a lollipop stick, or Stop–Children sign, then you must of course stop.

So there you have it. There is a lot in this section about sharing the road and how you can be a risk both to yourself and to other road users. As I have already said, you can do much to reduce this risk. You simply need to recognise where the risks lie, and the types of conditions, vehicles and road

users that can potentially increase these risks. You spot the risky situation, you assess it and you adjust your speed accordingly. It is up to you to decide how you deal with things. Just remember – your ability to take appropriate action lies in the speed at which you are driving your car.

Accidents

I need to say something about accidents and what you should do if you have a prang with someone else, or if you come across an accident that has already happened.

The first thing to tell you is that if you are involved in an accident, you are obliged to stop. Switch off the engine and decide whether you need to warn other traffic of the obstruction. If you are on a country road or a motorway, have just come round a bend or over the brow of a hill, or if it is night time, a warning triangle would be very useful to other motorists. You should always carry one of these in your car in case of accident or breakdown. On a dual carriageway or motorway you put the triangle at least 150 metres from the back of your car. On any other road it need only go 50 metres from the car but make sure it will be seen in plenty of time. This might mean placing it just before a bend if there isn't sufficient distance in which to warn traffic of an accident once they are round the bend. Use your hazard warning lights as well.

Try and note any witnesses. In the case that someone volunteers to act as a witness, take their details. Call the emergency services if necessary. If anyone has been injured, you must report the accident in person to the police as soon as possible and in any case within 24 hours. Providing there are no injuries, you only need to exchange details with the other parties involved. For insurance purposes make sure you write everything down. You need to get the following details from the other driver:

- Name, address and telephone number
- Make of car and registration number
- Insurance details – remember to check whether the driver is the owner of the vehicle or not.

You should also make notes on:

- Damage to vehicles and injuries to people
- Road and weather conditions at the time of the accident
- Details of the other vehicles involved, such as the colours, conditions, whether lights were on or indicators flashing, and so on
- ID numbers of police involved.

If you happen to have a camera with you, photos could be useful. You

Where an accident has occurred, a warning triangle is very useful to other motorists.

could also do with sketching a map showing the direction of travel of the vehicles involved, any street names, speed limits, skid marks, etc.

I know all this sounds a lot, but if your insurance company is going to settle all the costs then they are going to want as many of the facts as you can give them. Details such as the weather conditions, or whether another vehicle was signalling at the correct time, are all crucial to determining the outcome of an insurance claim. Don't forget that there are a lot of mitigating factors to consider and, regardless of how guilty you personally feel about the accident, you might not have actually caused it. If the other driver, for example, has been drinking and is over the legal limit

then he or she is to blame, not you. So don't be tempted to admit liability if you don't know the whole story.

Finally, it is very worthwhile to remember that you could be suffering from shock; so even if you feel uninjured, consider getting yourself checked up at the hospital.

You may need to make a statement to the police. You do not have to do this straightaway, and you may prefer to write one later and take it into the station – but keep a copy if you do.

At the scene of an accident

If you happen upon an accident that has only just occurred, don't rush in fearlessly. There's no point endangering yourself through possible collision from

other vehicles or from a fire that may not yet have taken hold.

Try to make the area as safe as possible by switching off the engine, stubbing out any cigarettes and warning other traffic. Call the emergency services if necessary and wait on the scene for them to arrive.

Knowledge of first-aid, even a little, might save somebody's life, provided you have the confidence to use it and know your limitations. You cannot, for example, match the ambulance team in expertise. Often, the most crucial thing you can do is offer reassurance to the injured. But you may need to do more, so let me explain a few of the most important things.

Don't move any casualties unless you think the car is going to explode. Don't attempt to remove an unconscious motorcyclist's helmet as

you could cause serious damage to the neck and spine.

Remember your **ABC**.

- **A** stands for 'airway'.
When you are with an unconscious person who has stopped breathing, the first thing to do is check their airway is clear. Gently tip their head back. This in itself could be enough to start the casualty breathing again. If it doesn't, turn their head to one side (unless you suspect a neck fracture) and hook out any blockages such as vomit, chewing gum or false teeth. Once the person starts breathing, place them in the recovery position and wait for help.

- **B** stands for 'breathing'.
If the person doesn't start breathing, and you have cleared the airway, you need to give mouth-to-mouth resuscitation. Provided that breathing returns, replace them in the recovery position.

- **C** stands for 'circulation'.
Check for a pulse. If you are sure there is no pulse you need to restore one by giving chest compressions and mouth-to-mouth ventilation in combination.

Pressing down on someone's heart if you haven't got a clue what you are doing could very easily cause more damage than good. So you should really read up on first-aid or enrol on one of the many first-aid courses run around the country by The British Red Cross, the St. John Ambulance Association and Brigade, and St. Andrew's Ambulance Association.

You may need to deal with other injuries, including bleeding, burns and shock.

In the case of bleeding, lay the casualty down and raise the wound above the heart. Apply downward pressure to the wound with, if possible, a clean dressing or pad. Take care not to press on anything which might be caught in the wound. Maintain pressure for up to 10 minutes until the blood clots naturally. Secure a pad with a length of cloth or bandage around the wound.

When dealing with burns and scalds the objective is to minimise injury and shock. Only tackle life-threatening burns and scalds. Burns and scalds to the throat, for example, can produce rapid swelling which may cause suffocation. Douse the affected areas with plenty of cold water and submerge under water for at least 10 minutes. Try to remove rings, watches and tight clothing from the affected area before any swelling might develop. Protect the wound with some clean cloth. You can use any other harmless cold liquid – such as milk – if there is no water.

If you suspect someone to be suffering from shock, lay the casualty down, raise their feet and turn their head to one side. Reassure them, keep them warm and don't give them anything to eat or drink. Wait for the ambulance to arrive.

Example Theory Test Questions

1. You are positioned and ready to reverse into a side road. You notice a pedestrian who may cross behind you. You should:

Mark one answer

○ a. sound your horn to warn the pedestrian to wait

○ b. wave the pedestrian across

✓ c. give way and wait to see if the pedestrian crosses

○ d. reverse quickly so as not to hold the pedestrian up

2. The age group most likely to be involved in a road accident is:

Mark one answer

✓ a. 17–25 year olds

○ b. 36–45 year olds

○ c. 46–55year olds

○ d. 55 year olds and over

3. During the daytime you should use dipped headlights:

Mark one answer

○ a. when reversing

✓ b. when visibility is poor

○ c. when driving along country roads

○ d. at all times

4. Your vehicle's stability can be affected by crosswinds. This is most likely when driving on:

Mark one answer

✓ a. an open stretch of road

○ b. a busy stretch of road

○ c. a narrow country lane

○ d. a long, straight road

5. To move off safely from a parked position you should always:

Mark one answer

○ a. use your indicators

✓ b. look in your mirrors and look round for a final check

○ c. give a hand signal

○ d. signal before you check your mirror

6. A driver is involved in an accident which causes damage only to his own vehicle. He should report this accident to the police:

Mark one answer

✓ a. within 24 hours

○ b. within 48 days

○ c. within 7 days

✓ d. not at all

7. You are least likely to be affected by crosswinds if you are:

Mark one answer

- a. riding a bicycle
- ✓ b. driving a car
- c. driving a high-sided vehicle
- d. riding a motorbike

8. You are approaching a right-hand bend. You should normally keep well to the:

Mark one answer

- a. right to avoid loose gravel at the edge of the road
- b. right to reduce the sharpness of the bend
- c. left to enable faster cornering
- ✓ d. left for a better view around the bend

9. You are driving along a motorway. It is raining and causing surface spray. You should:

Mark one answer

- ✓ a. use your headlights
- b. use your hazard warning lights
- c. use your fog lights
- d. use sidelights only

10. You are driving down a country road. Which of the following – possibly coming towards you on your side of the road – do you particularly need to be looking out for?

Mark one answer

- a. horse riders
- b. bicycles
- c. motorcycles
- ✓ d. pedestrians

11. You accelerate your car too harshly and it starts to skid. Your first action should be to:

Mark one answer

- ✓ a. ease off the accelerator
- b. brake gently
- c. steer into the skid
- d. brake hard

12. You are involved in an accident and a third party is injured. You are unable to produce your insurance certificate at the time of the accident. You must report the accident to the police within:

Mark one answer

- ✓ a. 24 hours
- b. 48 hours
- c. 7 days
- d. 14 days

13. While you are driving along, you see a pedestrian who is carrying a white stick with two red reflective bands. That person is likely to be:

Mark one answer
- ✓ a. blind and deaf
- ○ b. deaf without speech
- ○ c. blind and have difficulty walking
- ○ d. an orange badge scheme holder

14. When you drive around a bend, the speed of your vehicle should be slowest as you:

Mark one answer
- ✓ a. enter the bend
- ○ b. travel around the bend
- ○ c. travel around the second half of the bend
- ○ d. emerge from the bend

15. A pedestrian is hit by a car which is travelling at 40mph. The pedestrian:

Mark one answer
- ○ a. will certainly survive
- ○ b. will certainly be killed
- ○ c. will probably survive
- ✓ d. will probably be killed

16. When travelling at night in fog, and following another vehicle, you should:

Mark one answer
- ✓ a. keep a gap so that you can pull up safely if necessary
- ○ b. keep a gap that just allows you to see the tail lights of the vehicle in front
- ○ c. drive with your headlights on full beam to alert the driver to your presence
- ○ d. use only sidelights to avoid dazzle

17. When you drive on icy roads, the distance it normally takes to stop in an emergency on a dry road is likely to be increased:

Mark one answer
- ○ a. 2 times
- ○ b. 3 times
- ○ c. 5 times
- ✓ d. 10 times

18. Icy roads are often more slippery:

Mark one answer
- ○ a. in early spring
- ○ b. after it has been freezing for quite some time
- ○ c. in the north
- ✓ d. as it starts to thaw

19. While driving along the nearside lane of a two-lane motorway, you notice that you are being overtaken very slowly by a large goods vehicle. You should:

Mark one answer

○ a. accelerate sufficiently to allow the overtaking vehicle to pull in behind you

○ b. sound your horn to warn the driver you are there

○ c. keep a steady speed and allow the driver of the other vehicle to decide what action to take

✓ d. slow down so the vehicle can overtake more easily

20. When travelling down a long, steep hill you should control the speed of your vehicle by:

Mark one answer

○ a. using the foot brake all the way down

✓ b. selecting a lower gear on approach and using the foot brake

○ c. using the foot brake and selecting a lower gear on the way down

○ d. using the foot brake and selecting neutral

21. When cornering on snow or ice you should:

Mark one answer

○ a. change to a lower gear

✓ b. reduce speed

✓ c. keep a constant speed and use the highest gear possible

○ d. increase speed and change to a higher gear

22. You are approaching a junction and wish to turn right into it. The first action you should take is to:

Mark one answer

○ a. give a slowing down signal

○ b. brake

✓ c. check the mirrors

○ d. indicate right

23. When driving at night on an unlit road, you are dazzled by the headlights of an oncoming vehicle. You should:

Mark one answer

○ a. flash the main beam of your headlights

✓ b. slow down and stop if necessary

○ c. look to the left of the road

○ d. do an emergency stop

24. It is recommended that the right-hand lane of a three-lane motorway should be used by a driver:

Mark one answer

○ a. to maintain normal progress

○ b. for driving at high speed

○ c. at any time

Ⓥ d. for overtaking only

25. When turning right at a crossroads, where opposing vehicles are also turning right, extra dangers are involved when vehicles pass:

Mark one answer

○ a. offside-to-offside

○ b. nearside-to-offside

Ⓥ c. nearside-to-nearside

○ d. offside-to-nearside

26. You see a flashing amber light on a vehicle. This light indicates:

Mark one answer

Ⓥ a. a slow-moving vehicle

○ b. a fast-moving emergency vehicle

○ c. a Diplomatic vehicle

○ d. a doctor attending an emergency

27. When passing stationary vehicles you should, if possible, allow:

Mark one answer

Ⓥ a. at least the width of a car door

○ b. no less than 2 metres

○ c. no less than 3 metres

○ d. no more than a door's width

28. If you break down on a level crossing, your first action should be to:

Mark one answer

○ a. phone the signalman

○ b. push the vehicle clear of the crossing

Ⓥ c. get all passengers out of the vehicle and clear of the crossing

○ d. bump start your vehicle

29. After a long, dry spell, a road is likely to be most slippery:

Mark one answer

Ⓥ a. five minutes after it starts raining

○ b. after two hours of rain

○ c. when it has stopped raining

○ d. two hours after it has stopped raining

Answers and Explanations

1. c.
2. a.
3. b.
4. a.
5. b. is correct as that is the only sequence you always need.
6. d. is correct. The only damage is yours – nobody is hurt.
7. b.
8. d. is correct. You can see further round the bend if you keep to the left.
9. a.
10. d. is correct. Where there is no footpath, pedestrians are advised to walk on the right-hand side of the road so that they can see oncoming traffic.
11. a. is correct. Your first action should be to remove the cause of the skid, which in this case is too much acceleration.
12. a. is correct. You must report the accident within 24 hours, although you have 7 days to produce your insurance certificate.
13. a.
14. a.
15. d.
16. a.

17. d.
18. d.
19. d.
20. b. is correct. 'a' might overheat the brakes, and 'c' is too late to change gears.
21. c.
22. c.
23. b.
24. d.
25. c.
26. a. is correct. Emergency services use blue lights and doctors use green.
27. a.
28. c.
29. a. is correct. All the dirt, oil and grease on the road mix up with the raindrops and make the road very slippery. After a while much of the mess is washed away.

3. The Road

Introduction

The purpose of the *Highway Code* is to prevent accidents by having everyone adopt the same rules and regulations. It is there to make life easier by giving information, warning of problems and telling us what we can and cannot do. It creates uniformity in the way people act.

I now want to bring the *Highway Code* to life by taking you on a series of short imaginary drives. In each section – Town, Country and Motorway – I shall be in the passenger seat, explaining to you the rules and regulations governing the types of roads you are on. I will introduce you to the signs, markings, signals, rights of way and speed limits you come across and discuss the restrictions and limitations in force.

First, here is a short cut to learning. Remember the few simple pieces of information on this page, and you will find that you can often work out the meaning of a road sign. There are three

basic shapes of sign: circles, triangles and rectangles.

Circles give orders, triangles give warnings, rectangles give information.

Different colours are used to make signs even easier to remember:

Blue circles tell you what you MUST DO; red rings tell you what you MUST NOT DO.

Rectangles: blue give general information; green give route directions on primary roads; white with black borders give route directions on non-primary roads.

Motorway signs are slightly different, but I will explain more about that later on.

Town Driving

Journey One

Having settled yourself into the car and checked the seat belts, hand brake and gear lever, you start the engine. Looking in your mirrors and over your right shoulder into the blind spot, you see no reason to signal. There are no pedestrians or vehicles in sight, so just release the hand brake and move away – taking up a normal driving position about a metre from the kerb.

Straightaway you are going to take the first road on the right. A glance into your mirrors tells you it is safe to signal, and you position the car just to the left of the centre line. The road you are turning into has road humps all the way

Humps for ½ mile

along it to force everyone to drive slowly. There is also a 20mph zone sign at the start of the road to prevent drivers speeding between the humps.

At the end of this road is a sign telling you the 20mph zone has ended and that the speed limit is 30mph. You are now on a road with a great many parked cars and several side roads. As you have to turn left shortly, you are keeping an eye on what is happening behind and travelling fairly slowly. You see a

junction on the left and nearly turn into it, before noticing the No Entry sign.

You take the next available road on the left instead. Approaching the end of the road, you see a Stop sign and a solid white line and, after obeying the sign, turn right out of it. There is always a reason for having a Stop sign at a junction.

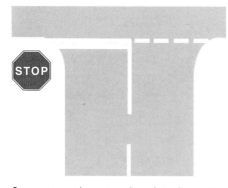

Sometimes there is a bend in the main road which takes it out of sight. If you are turning into a road such as this you must allow for cars driving too fast around this bend as they may suddenly come up behind you as you turn into the main road.

Having turned right and come

round the bend, you take the next road on the left. This is a one-way street so you can be in any lane you want – though you should not swerve

erratically from one to another. However, as you know you're going to be turning right at the end of this road, normally you would position yourself in the right-hand lane. But first you overtake a car crawling along at less than 20mph. Because it is a one-way street you can, of course, overtake on the left and then move into the right-hand lane.

At the end of the road is a sign informing you that two-way traffic crosses this one-way street. Now you know you have to turn onto the left-hand side of the road.

There's a warning sign of traffic lights ahead so check your mirrors in case you need to brake. You also need to bear in mind that this could be a warning sign either for a junction controlled by lights or for a pedestrian-crossing controlled by lights. In any event prepare to slow down and stop if necessary. As you round the bend, you see a sign telling you that the

lights are out of order. There is a queue of traffic ahead edging forwards through a fairly busy junction, and a policewoman controlling

the traffic. Put the palm of your left hand up at the windscreen to let her know you intend going straight ahead. She now beckons you through whilst telling oncoming traffic to stop. (You can study the signals a traffic controller can give, and the signals you need to be able to give to indicate your direction, in your copy of the *Highway Code*.)

There is a T-junction sign ahead and you want to go right. This is an interesting sign; as you get closer you can see a thick black line going to the right and a thin line to the left. This lets you know that this is a sharp bend to the right with a side road coming off to the left. As you are on the priority bend you don't need to signal; but if someone waiting to emerge looks like they might pull out in front of you because they think you're turning off to the left, you could give a right indicator just to confirm where you are going.

Looking well down the road, you see a crossroads warning sign. The thick black line tells you that you're on the priority road. Junctions are notorious accident blackspots and you

will see a lot of these signs. Never assume that drivers in side roads will see you. They may very well emerge without looking or they may look and misjudge the gap.

You see a car waiting in the road on the left. It is safe behind and you are easing off the gas. A glance to the right tells you the road on that side is clear and now you see that the driver on the left is looking your way. It seems safe to carry on.

You are now approaching a set of lights and a box junction. You are aware that you may not enter the junction – that is, cross the stop line – unless your exit is clear. If you want to turn right, you can sit in the box

and wait for a gap in the oncoming traffic, provided that your exit is clear. However, you aren't turning right here, but going straight on. The lights are green. Looking ahead, you can see the traffic backed up because of roadworks. You can just see a roadworks warning sign.

You check behind and slow down, stopping behind the line so as not to enter the box junction. The traffic to the left is now moving, so – making sure there is no cyclist coming up on your left – you can steer round the corner. And there, coming up on the left, is our first destination. ■

Without understanding the signs and the system, big roundabouts can appear more terrifying than they are.

Journey Two

I shall pick a different route to get us back. There will be a horrendous roundabout for you to cope with and several signs specifically related to cyclists.

We join a short stretch of one-way road leading up to a mini-roundabout, marked by a blue circular sign. You note the broken Give Way line at the entrance to the mini-roundabout; when we come up to the next, larger roundabout you will see that the line  at the mini-roundabout has smaller white markings. Although you are going straight ahead at this junction, you give way to the right. The road to the right is clear, so you emerge onto the roundabout – avoiding the markings in the middle – and leave at the second exit. You needn't signal because it is fairly tight; there isn't always enough time to signal left when leaving a mini-roundabout.

We are now coming up to that roundabout. You want to turn right, which means approaching in the right-hand lane and leaving in the left. This is not easy when there are lights and at least three lanes – sometimes four – all the way around the roundabout to deal with. The only saving grace is that the roundabout is well marked out. Watch other drivers carefully; invariably someone will realise they are in the wrong lane at the last moment and try to cut across the front of you. The secret to negotiating any big roundabout successfully is your speed; take your time and everything tends to fall smoothly into place.

There is an advance warning sign 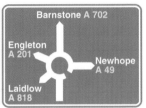 on the approach, clearly showing the layout and the route directions. There is also a sign indicating the appropriate lanes for the route directions. Checking behind that  it's safe, you signal right and position your car in the right-hand lane. The lights on the approach are green and the traffic to your right has stopped so you join the roundabout.

You want the fourth exit. You can't cut across two lanes at the last moment to leave, so somewhere between the first and third exits you need to change lanes and move into the middle one. But it's too late now; the next set of lights has turned to red. You are still in the right-hand lane, signalling right. As the lights change to green, you pull away. Checking your left-door mirror, you see it is safe to move into the middle lane. You cancel your right signal and steer to the left. As you pass the third exit – the exit before the one you want – check your mirrors, particularly the left. A quick glance over the left shoulder, then signal left and move decisively into the left-hand lane, before leaving the roundabout with a real feeling of satisfaction.

It is important to show cyclists great consideration. Ahead of you is a bridge, wide enough for two streams of traffic but not for cyclists as well. You see a sign prohibiting cyclists and a plate beneath telling them to dismount.

On the other side of the bridge there is a sign indicating a recommended route for cyclists. And  further on there is a with-flow bus and cycle lane. Bus lanes cause no end of problems to drivers. Just make sure you

look for the plate at the beginning telling you if and when other vehicles can use them.

down to 30. It is easy to miss this 30mph sign, though the absence of any further speed limit signs and the presence of street lighting should indicate that you are in a 30mph zone.

Some are in operation 24 hours of the day, while others can be used outside of rush hours. If you can't see a plate with times written on it then you should assume it operates as a bus lane continuously.

This bus lane tells you it is in operation between 7–10am. Since it is now early afternoon you can use it.

Looking ahead you see a pedestrian-crossing controlled by lights. As we are by a cycle route this is likely to be a Toucan crossing. As you draw closer you see that the lights, previously on red, have indeed just changed to red and amber (rather than the flashing amber you would expect at a Pelican crossing). Toucans are there for cyclists and pedestrians, and they permit cyclists to cross without dismounting as long as they wait for the green cycle symbol to show.

You are now approaching a 40mph speed limit zone. Fairly soon this drops back

Turning into your road you need to look for somewhere to park. There is a solid yellow line all the way down the left-hand side of the road. If you slow down you can read the accompanying plate, telling you there is no parking Monday to Saturday between 8am and 6:30pm. This is no good to you since it's only 3pm. On the other side of the road is a blue sign showing you can park for one hour, Monday to Saturday between 8am and 6:30pm. When the time has expired you may not return to that road and park for another two hours. Since it's summertime it is fine to park on the right-hand side of the road. As soon as it gets dark, however, it is illegal to park facing against the direction of the traffic flow.

Do remember that I can't possibly show you every road marking and sign you will ever come across, and that it is important for you to study the *Highway Code* closely. You need to read up on speed limits, arm signals, all the junction signs, traffic-light sequences, blue circle signs for route directions, roundabouts, cyclists' signs, bus lanes and parking and loading restrictions. ■

Journey Three

Setting off, you see a steady stream of traffic in your mirror. At last there's a gap. You have another quick check all round. Signal on, if necessary. Hand brake off. Clutch up. You check your

Young people will be getting on and off.

mirror and apply more gas to get your speed up to that of the rest of the traffic.

At the end of the road is a Give Way line, a painted triangle in the road

and an upside-down triangle saying Give Way. The more markings you see on the road, the greater you should assume the risk to be. So some roads have no road markings, some just a double broken white line, while others also have the sign and painted triangle or Stop signs and road markings.

You turn into the road ahead and notice a bus with a yellow  school-bus sign in its rear window. Bear in mind that young people will be getting on and off this bus, and may dart across the road to talk to friends without looking.

On the left is a school warning sign

Patrol

SCHOOL — KEEP — CLEAR

with flashing amber lights. There will be a school-crossing patrol further along, probably round this corner, so check behind and ease off the gas in case you need to start braking as you round the bend. And there is the lollipop man just stepping into the road with his Stop Children sign. You obviously stop at this sign.

A little further on you see the school with the SCHOOL KEEP CLEAR yellow zigzag lines on the road. It's very busy here and the road is really quite narrow with cars parked left and right setting children down. You are in stop-start traffic and have to leave a gap before the next junction on the left so that other road users can turn into and out of it easily. A Keep Clear sign painted on the road tells you to keep the junction clear, but you should

WEAK BRIDGE

Priority over oncoming vehicles

remember not to block a side road like this in any case.

Further along this road much of the traffic disappears and we are now approaching a bridge. There was once a two-way road over the bridge but a sign now announces the bridge is weak and only single file traffic is allowed to cross. The road has been narrowed to the width of one vehicle and a sign is giving you priority over vehicles coming from the other direction.

Over the bridge a car slows down to let you come through first. You put up your hand to thank the driver. At the end of this road, if you turned round and had a look at the sign, you would see that because of the weak bridge, there is a weight restriction on the vehicles allowed to use it. No goods vehicles over a maximum gross weight of 7.5 tonnes permitted on this road.

You turn out of this road, and head towards a set of lights. There's a fair bit of traffic in this left-hand lane and we seem to be creeping along. The right-hand lane, however, doesn't look too bad at all. You need to decide whether you'd make better progress in the right lane, or whether you'd only get boxed in behind another vehicle waiting to turn right at the lights. Looking ahead, you see a No Right Turn sign. You check your mirror, signal right and move into the right-hand lane, overtaking all the other traffic held up because so many of them want to turn left at the lights.

At the junction there are route direction signs, black writing on a

Bramfield
B 1066

Oatham
B 1216

white background. This tells you that you're on a non-primary route (useful information perhaps if you were lost and trying to identify where you were on an Ordnance Survey map).

So that's it for town journeys. You will need to read up on the rest of the *Highway Code* signs and road markings to do with town driving. I can't mention every sign you might need to know in order to pass your Theory Test, but I can show you some pattern and method in the use of signs. Picturing signs in context can make them far easier to remember. ■

Country

Town
(traffic
jams)

Country Driving

I now want to show you the sort of signs and road markings you could expect to come across in the country.

It may be fairly obvious to you what many of these signs mean because of what you know already about town driving. Really, with the knowledge you've gained already, you should find that you can use your common sense to interpret most of the signs you haven't yet seen.

Journey One

Driving in the country can be a challenging test of your skill in handling a car. You need to read the road well enough ahead to plan your speed and position, anticipating and avoiding any problems that might arise.

The Five Habits are every bit as valuable in the country as they are in urban areas. In fact, because your speed can be as high as 60 or even 70mph on dual carriageways, the ability to look well ahead, move your eyes, spot the problems, keep space and be seen becomes absolutely crucial.

But for now, you are just leaving the town. You pass through a 40mph speed limit zone and now you hit the national speed limit. You expect to find speed limits going up as you head out of a built-up area and going down again as you near the next town or village. The national speed limit is:

■ 60mph on a single carriageway
■ 70mph on a dual carriageway.

(In a survey, drivers were quizzed on the national speed limit. Incredibly, 80 per cent did not know there are actually two national speed limits depending on the type of road you are on. And 70 per cent didn't even recall what the national speed limit sign looked like.)

You are now approaching a bend – in fact it's a double bend, the first to the right. A route deviation sign – with black and white chevrons – indicates that the bend is probably quite sharp.

You check behind you and start to brake. You need your speed to be at  its lowest – with the correct gear selected – before you get into the bend so that you can then gently accelerate through it and have the power to pull away once the bend is over.

You come out of the bends and you see the road straightens out. The road markings at this point are the usual centre lines (1). Further ahead a sign warns of a hidden dip, and the road markings have gone to two white lines with a solid white line on your side of the road (2). You may not cross this line unless it is to pass an obstruction, a cyclist, another vehicle travelling at less than 10mph or to turn into *(1)* a side road or driveway. Oncoming traffic can cross their broken white line if it is safe to do so.

As you get into the dip, the lines change to two solid white lines (3). Once out of the dip, a broken white line indicates you can overtake if it is safe; oncoming traffic, however, may not cross their solid white line (4). It is all to *(3)* do with visibility. You can see the road clearly enough as you come out of the dip to overtake if you wish, whereas oncoming drivers have poor visibility because the road falls away from their view.

A warning sign for horses leads you to expect riders and their mounts. In this situation you must slow right down before you get near them. Avoid revving the car or making sudden movements, and give them as much room as possible as you pass. You may come across a jumpy, easily startled horse, and you can't afford to take risks.

Hidden dip

(2)

(4)

You are now coming to a single track road. A sign warns that the road will narrow on both sides, and the accompanying plate tells you it is a

Single track road

single track road. It is easy to confuse this warning sign with the one that indicates a dual carriageway is coming to an end.

Now you are on the single track road, keep your eye out for passing places. If a car comes towards you and there isn't room to pass, you may have to reverse back to the last passing place you noticed.

There is a car now approaching, but fortunately there is a passing place on the right-hand side of the road. So slow down and stop virtually opposite this spot and allow the other driver to pull in and manoeuvre round you. ■

Journey Two

Almost immediately after setting out, you have a steep downhill gradient to deal with. A warning sign tells you we're approaching a 20 per cent gradient –

also known as a 1:5. This means that for every five feet you go forwards, the road drops one foot, so it's a fairly steep hill to cope with.

There is also a sign saying you should now be in

Low gear now

a low gear. You can't come down a long hill relying on your brakes to slow you down. Selecting a lower gear allows the engine to assist in holding the car back, preventing it from running away. If you keep your foot on the pedal over a long distance, your brakes may fail.

Now you pass a sign warning you that the rocks and cliffs at the side of the road are unsafe and you may come across falling (or fallen) rocks. This sign is a disclaimer only – it does not indicate any acceptance of responsibility.

Further on you see a sign warning of a slippery road surface. This can mean several things. The road surface might be exposed and prone to icing up in the winter or there could be a farm nearby. Tractors leave mud on the roads,

which could make the surface slippery if it's been raining. And cattle going to and from milking could leave cowpats on the road, which might cause you to skid. There could also be deciduous trees in the area and in the autumn wet leaves on the road are treacherous. So slow down at a sign like this and try and work out why it's there.

In this case, the next sign warns you of cattle. There is a farm nearby and, although there are no cattle being herded across the road, there is a tractor up ahead slowing down the traffic. The road is starting to widen and straighten out now so the two cars in front of us will get the chance to overtake the tractor in a moment.

Notice the hatch markings down the road surrounded by a broken white line. Because the line is broken you are allowed to enter the hatched area – provided it is safe. Up ahead is a staggered crossroads.

Ahead you see a sign warning of a hump bridge (not to be confused with the signs warning of an uneven road surface or road humps). This hump bridge must be fairly steep because a second sign warns of the risk of grounding.

Over the bridge another sign informs you there could be

pedestrians in the road as there is no footpath. Now here is a warning sign for a ford. You check behind that it is safe to slow down. The water is not too deep but, once through, do as the sign says and

test your brakes. To do this you drive slowly in first gear with your right foot on the accelerator and your left foot on the brake. This dries out the brakes if they got too wet coming through the ford.

Towards the end of this journey through the country, we come to a level crossing, so we'll spend some time concentrating on level crossings (though you can, of course, find these in towns too).

There are several types of level crossing, controlled in different ways. Some have gates and barriers, some have lights, and at others you make the decision to stop yourself.

On this occasion an advanced warning sign with a train on it informs us we are approaching a level crossing without a barrier or gate. Accompanying this sign

is one telling us that there are lights controlling the crossing. Because the crossing is concealed around the next bend there are also countdown markers.

You will only see markers like these – red lines on a white background – on the approach to a level crossing. They indicate the distance to the stop line.

As you come round the bend you see the crossing with the lights. These are off, indicating no train is coming – though you should still check to make sure before you come over the crossing.

If there is a steady amber light you should stop unless it is unsafe for you to do so. If flashing red lights are showing, you must stop.

As I said, there is no gate or barrier here and the St. Andrew's cross you can see confirms that. Most crossings these days have half or full barriers but you do still come across ones like this.

If you are waiting at a level crossing and the train goes by but the lights continue to flash, then it means another train will be coming soon. Obviously you must wait.

If your car breaks down on the crossing, the first thing you must do is get everyone out of the car. Then go and phone the signal operator who will tell you what to do next. Unless the alarm sounds or the amber light comes on, it may be possible to move the car clear of the crossing.

That covers level crossings. Do remember to read up on these in the *Highway Code*. Each sign has its own meaning and is giving you a piece of information peculiar to that particular type of crossing. ∎

Motorway Driving

Before setting out on our imaginary motorway journey there are several things you need to do first. Although your car should be serviced regularly, you still need to check the tyre pressures. Do this when the tyres are cold, or you will get a false reading once they warm up. And remember to fill the petrol tank. Also check the oil and make sure there is plenty of water in the radiator and in the windscreen washer bottle. Ensure your brake and clutch fluid reservoirs are full, your lights and indicators are all working and the glass is clear.

It is as well to plan your route in advance, work out which exit you need to take off the motorway, and even have a rough idea of where you can stop for a break if need be.

You must also hold a full driving licence for the vehicle you are driving. Learner drivers are not allowed on motorways, unless learning to drive a Large Goods Vehicle.

Certain types of vehicle are not allowed on motorways. Restrictions apply to the following:

■ Invalid carriages less than 254 kilogrammes in unladen weight
■ Pedal cycles
■ Motorcycles under 50cc engine capacity
■ Agricultural vehicles. (Imagine the chaos caused on busy motorways by slow-moving tractors, combine harvesters and so on)
■ Certain slow-moving vehicles carrying oversized loads (except by special permission).

You also need to know the restrictions that apply to the right-hand lane of motorways with three or more lanes.

None of the following are allowed to use the right-hand lane of a motorway:

■ A vehicle with a gross weight of more than 7.5 tonnes

- A bus longer than 12 metres
- A coach
- Any vehicle towing a trailer or a caravan.

There are also restrictions on the following:

- Stopping – and this includes stopping on the hard shoulder – except in an emergency
- U-turns
- Reversing (it seems almost impossible that anyone could decide to reverse on a motorway, even if they had missed their exit, yet I have seen this happen several times, once with very serious consequences)
- Animals and pedestrians
- Picking up hitch-hikers – you are also breaking the law if you stop on a slip road to give them a lift.

The journey

But now you see a motorway sign ahead. We have been following signs for the M100 for some time. These signs are rectangular with a green background (showing that they are information signs on a primary road). The part of the sign that says M100 is coloured blue to help you see it refers to a motorway – and the M100

appears in brackets. You spot a brown and white tourist sign telling you there

is an ancient monument off to the right, and for a moment you are tempted to follow this instead.

The sign ahead is different to the previous ones. The M100 part of the sign is still coloured blue, but is no longer in brackets. The motorway symbol indicates that motorway regulations start at the junction shown by the sign. You join the motorway at a roundabout junction, and you need to take the third exit straight ahead. This exit is a two-lane slip road. (A sign at

the entrance to the slip road is fortunately not lit up. If the lights were flashing and the lanes were lit up, it would mean all the lanes on the motorway were closed and we could not enter.) You head  down the slip road in the left-hand lane and you see hatch markings splitting the two lanes ahead. These help heavy volumes of traffic to join the motorway more easily. You are not allowed to drive over the markings to change lanes, so you stay in your lane and join the motorway where the markings end.

Remember that traffic on the motorway has priority; looking well ahead and using your mirrors to adjust your speed, you blend in with

the traffic and slip into a gap without causing other traffic to slow down. This is a three-lane motorway, but you stay in the left-hand lane for a while so you can adjust to the speed of the traffic.

You now increase your speed to the 70mph limit. Whenever it is safe, you overtake slower-moving vehicles by moving out to the middle or right-hand lane as necessary. Because of the high speed of other traffic, you use the Mirror Signal Manoeuvre sequence earlier than normal. You check your mirrors constantly to help you judge the speed of traffic catching you up from behind and to ensure that no vehicle has suddenly entered your blind spot.

You do your best not to drive in other people's blind spots. You certainly don't want anyone changing lanes and not realising you're alongside them. You are also only using the middle and right-hand lanes

Stay in your lane when you encounter splitter lanes.

for overtaking, pulling back into the left lane whenever it is safe to do so.

You keep a good distance from the cars in front – at least one metre for each mile per hour of speed. So at 70mph you are leaving at least 70 metres gap. Remember that you can check if the gap is safe by using the two-second rule. When you see the car in front pass under that bridge, you say out loud: 'Only a fool breaks the two-second rule.' If you finish saying this well before you reach the bridge, then your gap is safe.

Over on the hard shoulder, you see an emergency telephone.  These telephones are linked directly to the police and you will find one about every mile as you travel along. If you look a bit harder you will also spot a small blue and white marker post with a telephone and arrow on it. These occur about every 100 metres. The arrow shows you the direction in which you'll find the nearest telephone.

Remember that you can only stop on the hard shoulder in case of emergency. If you need to use the emergency telephone – because your car has broken down, say – you will be

asked to read out the number on the telephone box. This number helps the police tell exactly where you are. If you have an emergency warning triangle, place it on the hard shoulder at least 150 metres behind your car.

A sign now informs you there are roadworks two miles up ahead; as you know, roadworks often mean delays.

You see another sign about a mile from the problem, and now you need to be extra careful.

This sign warns of a temporary mandatory speed limit of 50mph in three-quarters of a mile, so you start reducing speed. The next sign tells you which lanes are closed; these usually appear 800, 600, 400 and

200 yards before the works, so there is little excuse for getting caught out at the last second. This sign tells you that the right-hand lane is closed, but that you can use the hard shoulder. There are signs to show you what lanes are available, which lane to use if you

wish to leave the motorway at a junction in the roadworks, and which to take if you want to carry on further.

Service areas usually occur at between 20- and 30-mile intervals on motorways, but do be warned that this is not always the case. Here is a sign for the next one, a mile away, and where you want to stop. By the half-mile sign

Services		
M100	EATWELL	1m
	FRAMPTON	22m
M27 (N)	NO SERVICES	
M27 (S)	SUNNYSIDE	6m

you should be in the left-hand lane, ready to signal and drive into the deceleration lane ahead. Looking ahead, you see the sign that tells you when the motorway regulations end.

You leave the services area with dipped headlights and rejoin the motorway from the slip road. Now it is getting dark, it is easier to see the different-coloured studs along the road. As you reach the end of the slip road, green studs show you where to rejoin the main carriageway of the motorway. White studs mark the lanes, red studs mark the left edge of the carriageway where it joins with the hard shoulder, and amber studs mark the edge of the central reservation. Exits and entrances from slip roads are marked by green studs. These coloured studs are

necessary in the dark, and particularly in poor visibility.

Junction 25 is now approaching (you

know this is the one you want, because you checked before setting out). The sign ahead – about a mile before the junction – gives only basic information, and your destination is not actually mentioned by name. Another sign

comes up, similar to the first but which includes the name of your destination, about half a mile from the exit. You move into the left-hand lane. Look to the left on the hard shoulder, and you'll see the countdown markers ahead. They mark the distance to the start of the deceleration lane, each bar representing about 100 metres.

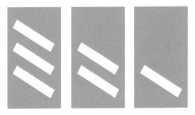

You see another destination sign at the start of the deceleration lane. You signal left between the three- and two-bar markers, check for other traffic leaving the motorway, steer into the deceleration lane and start to slow down.

The deceleration lane leads onto the slip road and, like so many others, it has several sharp bends. You slow

down enough to be able to cope easily. You see the end of motorway sign, and now you are back to driving on normal roads. You will probably feel as though you're driving much slower than you really are, so check your speedometer a few times until you get used to the new conditions. ■

Let me now remind you of a few motorway rules.

Speed limits on motorways

- Cars and motorcycles 70mph
- Cars towing caravans or trailers 60mph
- Buses and coaches .... 70mph (not exceeding 12 metres in length)
- Goods vehicles 70mph

(up to 7.5 tonnes, unless articulated or towing a trailer)
- Goods vehicles .... 60mph (over 7.5 tonnes)

Illuminated signals on motorways

Signals on motorways are located either at the back of the hard shoulder, on the central reservation, or on overhead gantries above the motorway.

The signals that you see at the back of the hard shoulder or on the central reservation apply to drivers in all lanes. The signals above the road apply only to drivers in the lane below that particular signal. These signals are turned off when conditions are normal. They are switched on by the police in an emergency – sometimes they are activated by weather conditions such as fog – and they tell you what to do or what to expect ahead.

Four amber lights flash horizontally in alternate pairs, drawing your attention to the message on the signal. Flashing red signals mean you must stop unless you can join another lane. Take great care when you see these signals lit up. You may not immediately see the reason for them, but there could be an accident blocking the road further ahead.

Hard Shoulder	Left-hand lane	Middle lane	Right-hand lane
Emergencies only. Never use the hard shoulder to overtake.	Use this lane unless overtaking. In an emergency it is much easier to reach the hard shoulder if you are driving next to it.	Use this lane to overtake traffic in the left-hand lane. You may stay in the middle lane if you are overtaking a line of slower-moving vehicles. This is safer than moving in and out repeatedly.	Use this lane to overtake traffic in the middle lane. Large Goods Vehicles (LGVs) and vehicles towing trailers are not allowed to use this lane if all three lanes are open.

Lane discipline   *DO NOT STRADDLE LANES*

I hope this section will help you remember the different signs, signals, rules and regulations that govern our use of roads. The more ways you find to study this essential knowledge, and the more opportunities you have to actually make use of it when driving, the easier you will find it all to keep in your head. Unfortunately you will have no chance to practise motorway driving until after your test but some of the following questions and the exercises relating to motorways on pages 138–139, together with their explanations, will help you retain the information.

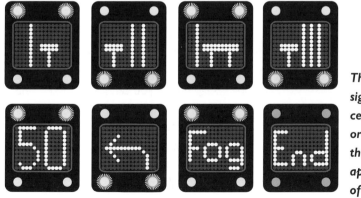

The illuminated signals on the central reservation or at the back of the hard shoulder apply to all lanes of the motorway.

Example Theory Test Questions

1. What does this sign mean?

Mark one answer

- a. narrow right-hand lane
- ✓ b. right-hand lane is closed
- c. no overtaking
- d. no right turn

2. Which sign means 'no overtaking'?

Mark one answer

 a.○

 b.○

 c.✓

 d.○

3. What does this sign mean?

Mark one answer

- a. cycle route
- ✓ b. ring road
- c. railway station
- d. roadworks

4. What does this sign mean?

Mark one answer

- a. pedestrian crossing
- b. no pavement
- c. pedestrian route
- ✓ d. no pedestrians

5. You see a traffic light ahead with amber lit up. Which light or lights will come on next?

Mark one answer

- a. green only
- ✓ b. red only
- c. red and amber together
- d. green and amber together

6. When driving along a road which is marked out for lanes of traffic, you should position your vehicle in the lane in which you are travelling:

Mark one answer

- a. on the white line
- ✓ b. in the middle
- c. well to the right
- d. well to the left

7. You should use the hard shoulder of a motorway to:

Mark one answer

- a. stop when you are tired
- b. overtake
- c. join the motorway
- d. stop in an emergency

8. You must not use your horn in a built-up area between:

Mark one answer

- a. 8pm and 7am
- b. 8pm and first light
- c. 11:30pm and 7am
- d. dark and 7:30am

9. On a three-lane motorway, you may overtake on the left:

Mark one answer

- a. when it is safe to do so and traffic in the lane to the right is moving more slowly than traffic in your lane
- b. at any time
- c. when travelling in queues of slow-moving traffic and the vehicles in the lanes to the right are moving at a slower speed
- d. only in an emergency

10. Traffic signs have been established on British roads for some time. The use of particular signs is dependent upon a system. It is true to say that, in general:

Mark one answer

- a. circles give orders, triangles warn and rectangles inform
- b. circles give orders, rectangles warn and triangles inform
- c. circles warn, triangles order and rectangles inform
- d. circles inform, triangles give orders and rectangles warn

11. Areas of white diagonal stripes painted on the road are to:

Mark one answer

- a. indicate no parking areas
- b. separate traffic streams liable to be a danger to each other, or protect traffic turning right
- c. allow for overtaking on narrow roads and protect traffic turning left
- d. reduce traffic speed on approach to roundabouts

12. You are driving along and see these road markings ahead. You are approaching:

Mark one answer
- ✓ a. a pedestrian-crossing
- ○ b. a box junction
- ○ c. an uneven road surface
- ○ d. an adverse road camber

13. What does this sign mean:

Mark one answer
- ○ a. pedal cyclists only
- ✓ b. no cycling
- ○ c. recommended route for pedal cyclists
- ○ d. warning, cyclists ahead

14. You are driving along a two-lane, one-way street and wish to turn right. Unless road markings tell you otherwise, you should position yourself:

Mark one answer
- ○ a. in the left-hand lane
- ✓ b. in the right-hand lane
- ○ c. just left of the centre of the road
- ○ d. in the lane with least traffic

15. A single, broken white line with long markings and short gaps in the middle of the carriageway means:

Mark one answer
- ○ a. do not cross
- ○ b. no overtaking
- ○ c. hazard warning
- ✓ d. centre line of road

16. The law requires you to turn on your lights:

Mark one answer
- ✓ a. at lighting-up time
- ○ b. when other drivers do so
- ○ c. between 11pm and 7:30am
- ○ d. before dark

17. You are driving along a motorway and see red flashing lights on the overhead gantry above your lane. You should:

Mark one answer
- ○ a. drive on in that lane until more information is available
- ○ b. drive onto the hard shoulder
- ○ c. stop
- ✓ d. drive no further in that lane

18. This sign means:

Mark one answer

- ☑ a. national speed limit applies
- ○ b. end of speed limit
- ○ c. travel at any speed
- ○ d. clearway, no stopping

19. You are driving along but can see no speed limit sign. You can tell that the limit is 30mph by noticing:

Mark one answer

- ○ a. the pedestrian crossing ahead
- ○ b. hazard warning lines
- ☑ c. that street lights are less than 200 metres apart
- ○ d. red reflectors mark the left side of the carriageway

20. On a three-lane motorway the left-hand lane may be used by:

Mark one answer

- ☑ a. any vehicle allowed to use the motorway
- ○ b. large vehicles only
- ○ c. emergency vehicles only
- ○ d. slow vehicles only

21. You are driving down a road which is only wide enough for one vehicle. You see a car coming towards you. What TWO actions should you take?

Mark two answers

- ○ a. wait opposite a passing place on your left
- ☑ b. wait opposite a passing place on your right
- ○ c. drive to the right-hand passing space and wait
- ☑ d. pull into a passing place on your left
- ○ e. encourage the other driver to reverse
- ○ f. only give way to a larger vehicle

22. Coloured, reflecting road studs may be used with white lines on roads. Green studs may be used:

Mark one answer

- ☑ a. across lay-bys or side roads
- ○ b. to mark the left-hand edge of the carriageway
- ○ c. to mark the central reservation of a dual carriageway
- ○ d. to mark sharp bends

23. You wish to cross a dual carriageway with a wide central reservation. To go straight ahead, you should:

Mark one answer
- ⬤ a. treat each half of the carriageway as a separate road
- ◯ b. assume priority over the second carriageway once committed
- ◯ c. always wait until both carriageways are clear
- ◯ d. turn left and then right at the first safe opportunity

24. What does a sign with white writing and a brown background show?

Mark one answer
- ◯ a. primary route
- ⬤ b. tourist direction
- ◯ c. minor route
- ◯ d. motorway route

25. This sign means:

Mark one answer
- ◯ a. steep hill downwards
- ⬤ b. steep hill upwards
- ◯ c. height limit
- ◯ d. weight limit

26. You are travelling along a two-way road where the carriageway is marked for three lanes of traffic. You should use the centre lane:

Mark one answer
- ◯ a. on the assumption that you have priority over oncoming vehicles
- ⬤ b. on the assumption that you have no more right to be there than a vehicle coming from the opposite direction
- ⬤ c. only to overtake very slow-moving vehicles
- ◯ d. only to avoid roadworks or other obstructions

27. You may park on the right-hand side of the road at night:

Mark one answer
- ◯ a. facing against the direction of the traffic flow
- ⬤ b. on a one-way street
- ◯ c. in a road with street lighting
- ◯ d. anywhere more than 10 metres from a junction

Answers and Explanations

1. b.
2. c.
   a. is priority over vehicles from the opposite direction.
   b. is no motor vehicles.
   d. is two-way traffic.
3. b.
4. d. is correct. Remember, red circles or rings tell you what you must not do.
5. b. is correct. Traffic lights go: red, red with amber, green, amber, red.
6. b.
7. d.
8. c.
9. c.
10. a.
11. b.
12. a.
13. b. is correct. Red circles normally say 'no'. The same picture in blue means route for pedal cycles only. In a red triangle it warns of a pedal cycle route ahead.

14. b.
15. c.
16. a. The legal time varies according to the time of year.
17. d.
18. a.

19. c.
20. a.
21. b. and d.
22. a.
23. a.
24. b.
25. b. is correct. You always read from left to right, so if the numbers are climbing the hill sign from left to right, it's an uphill gradient.
26. b.
27. b. The reflectors on your car need to be seen by traffic on your side of the road, so a one-way street is the only safe place to park on the right at night.

Test Your Knowledge – Picture Quiz
Roundabouts
Answers and explanations on page 140

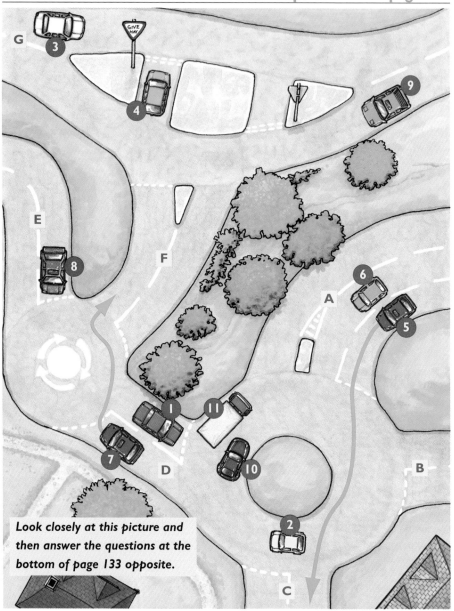

Look closely at this picture and then answer the questions at the bottom of page 133 opposite.

Parking

Look at this picture then, (below on the right), tick YES or NO according to whether you think the vehicle is correctly parked.

Roundabouts (left)	YES/NO
1. Should 1 give way to 2?	✓
2. Should 3 give way to 4?	✓
3. Should 5 signal left here if taking road B?	✓
4. Should 6 signal right here if taking road D?	✓
5. Should 5 take the blue line if taking road C?	✓ ✓
6. Should 2 signal left here if taking road D?	✓
7. Should 7 take the blue line to reach road F? ...	✓
8. Should 8 signal here if taking road D?	✓
9. Should 9 signal if taking road G?	✓
10. Should 10 overtake 11?	✓

Parking	YES/NO
1.	✓
2.	✓
3.	✓
4.	✓
5.	✓
6.	✓
7.	✓
8.	✓
9.	✓
10.	✓

Overtaking

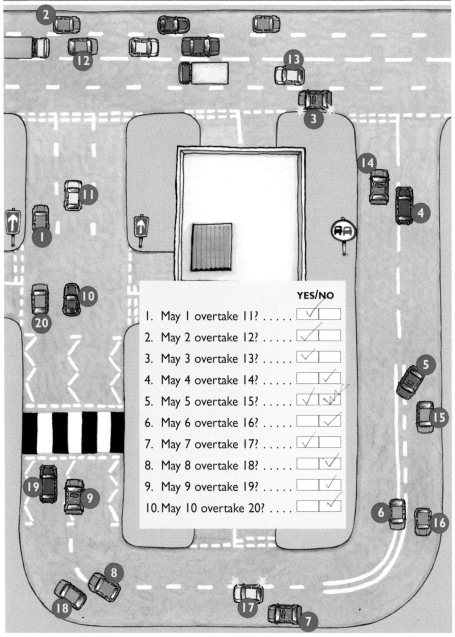

	YES/NO
1. May 1 overtake 11?	YES ✓
2. May 2 overtake 12?	YES ✓
3. May 3 overtake 13?	YES ✓
4. May 4 overtake 14?	NO ✓
5. May 5 overtake 15?	YES ✓ NO
6. May 6 overtake 16?	NO ✓
7. May 7 overtake 17?	YES ✓
8. May 8 overtake 18?	NO ✓
9. May 9 overtake 19?	NO ✓
10. May 10 overtake 20?	NO ✓

Positioning

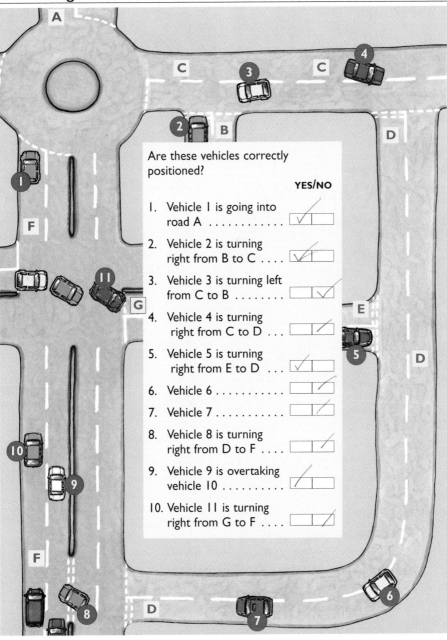

Are these vehicles correctly positioned?

YES/NO

1. Vehicle 1 is going into road A . . . . [✓]

2. Vehicle 2 is turning right from B to C . . . . [✓]

3. Vehicle 3 is turning left from C to B . . . . [ ][✓]

4. Vehicle 4 is turning right from C to D . . . [ ][✓]

5. Vehicle 5 is turning right from E to D . . . [✓]

6. Vehicle 6 . . . . [ ][✓]

7. Vehicle 7 . . . . [ ][✓]

8. Vehicle 8 is turning right from D to F . . . . [ ][✓]

9. Vehicle 9 is overtaking vehicle 10 . . . . [✓]

10. Vehicle 11 is turning right from G to F . . . . [ ][✓]

Junctions

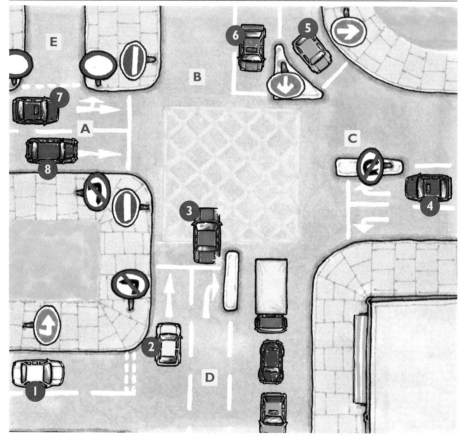

		YES/NO	
1.	May vehicle 1 turn right at road D?		✓
2.	May vehicle 2 turn left in to road A?		✓
3.	Should vehicle 3 have entered box junction to turn into road C?	✓	
4.	May vehicle 4 make a U-turn back along road C?		✓
5.	May vehicle 5 turn left into road C?	✓	
6.	May vehicle 6 turn left into road C?		✓
7.	May vehicle 6 enter box junction to go ahead into road D?		✓
8.	May vehicle 7 turn left into road E?		✓
9.	May vehicle 7 turn left into road B?	✓	
10.	May vehicle 8 turn right into road D?	✓	✓

Level crossings

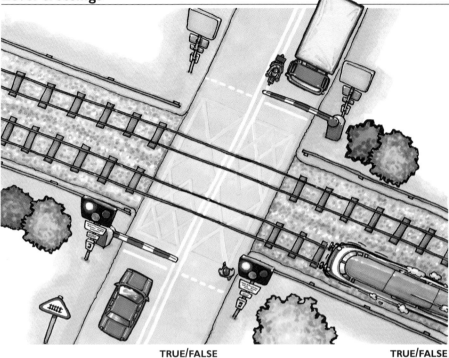

TRUE/FALSE

1. After the amber lights flash and the alarm sounds, the barriers come down ......

2. Drivers of large or slow vehicles must phone the signalman and get permission to cross ....

3. If you stall or break down on the crossing, get your passengers to help push your vehicle clear ....

4. Some crossings with lights do not have barriers ....

5. If the barriers stay down and the lights continue to flash, it means another train is coming ....

TRUE/FALSE

6. If, after about 3 minutes, the barriers stay down, you may zigzag around them ....

7. You should not enter the yellow box unless there is enough clear road beyond the crossing for your vehicle ...

8. If you do telephone the signalman before crossing, phone again afterwards to let him know you are over ....

9. Red flashing lights mean stop ....

10. Always give way to a train ..

Motorway regulations

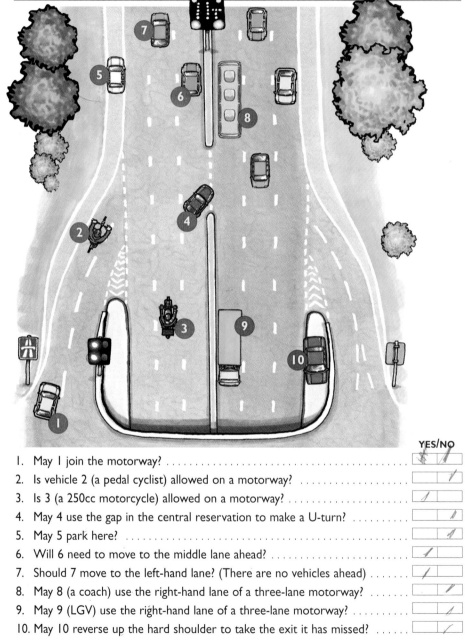

YES/NO

1. May I join the motorway? ....

2. Is vehicle 2 (a pedal cyclist) allowed on a motorway? ....

3. Is 3 (a 250cc motorcycle) allowed on a motorway? ....

4. May 4 use the gap in the central reservation to make a U-turn? ....

5. May 5 park here? ....

6. Will 6 need to move to the middle lane ahead? ....

7. Should 7 move to the left-hand lane? (There are no vehicles ahead) ....

8. May 8 (a coach) use the right-hand lane of a three-lane motorway? ....

9. May 9 (LGV) use the right-hand lane of a three-lane motorway? ....

10. May 10 reverse up the hard shoulder to take the exit it has missed? ......

Motorways

Match the numbers on the diagram to the items listed below.

Example: the correct sign for 'Start of motorway regulations' is numbered 8 on the diagram.
So put 8 in the square like this:

Start of motorway regulations? 8

Now see how many you can identify:

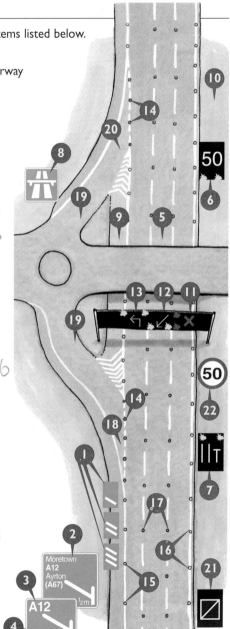

Right-hand lane closed 7

Acceleration lane 20

Main carriageway 5

Hard shoulder 9

Central reservation 10

Slip road 19

Deceleration lane 18

Advisory speed limit 50mph 6

Countdown markers 1

1 mile to exit 3

Leave at next exit 13

Half mile to next exit 2

Do not go further in this lane 11

Exit number 4

Change lane 12

Red coloured studs 15

Green coloured studs 14

Amber coloured studs 16

White coloured studs 17

Compulsory speed limit 50mph 22

End of restriction 21

Picture quiz answers and explanations

Roundabouts – page 132

1. Yes. The general rule at roundabouts is give way to traffic from the right.
2. No. The road markings indicate that vehicle 4 should give way. In this situation vehicle 4 gives way on the roundabout.
3. Yes. Vehicle 5 should signal left on the approach and through the roundabout.
4. Yes. Vehicle 6 should signal right on the approach and change to a left signal when it reaches the position of 2.
5. No. Vehicle 5 should keep to the left through the roundabout. This would allow vehicle 6 to take the inside route for turning right.
6. Yes. Signal left when passing the exit before the one you want to take.
7. No. Even if the disc is only a mini-roundabout painted on the road, vehicle 7 should try to go around it.
8. No. Vehicle 8 is going straight over, so should only signal as it passes road F, if at all.
9. No. A right signal might make others think vehicle 9 was going where vehicle 4 is. A left-turn signal would be taken to mean going to road F. To avoid misleading signals, it would be safer not to signal.
10. No. Long vehicles may need all the available space to negotiate the roundabout.

Parking – page 133

1. No. Blocking hospital entrance.
2. Yes. This sign shows that pavement parking is permitted.
3. Yes. The bus lane isn't operating at the time of day shown on the clock.
4. No. Parking is not permitted where there are double white lines in the middle of the road.
5. No. Double yellow lines on the road mean waiting restrictions; the plate says No Waiting at any time.
6. No. Parking at junctions makes it difficult for other road users to see each other.
7. Yes. There are waiting restrictions, but not for the time of day shown.
8. No. Not during the working day, unless a time plate states otherwise.
9. No. Not on the pavement.
10. No. It is an offence to park on the zigzag lines at pedestrian crossings.

Overtaking – page 134

1. Yes. In a one-way street, you may overtake on either side.
2. Yes. When traffic is moving in queues, the left lane may move quicker than the right.
3. Yes. If you are turning left, then you may overtake on the left.
4. No. There is a No Overtaking sign which prohibits this.
5. Yes. The broken white line is on 5's side of the road, so overtaking is permitted.
6. No. 6 is crossing a solid line to overtake; this is prohibited.
7. Yes. 7 may overtake on the left because 17 is indicating a right turn.
8. No. Although not prohibited, it is not advisable to overtake on a bend.
9. No. It is an offence to overtake the leading vehicle when approaching a pedestrian crossing.
10. No. Although not prohibited, it is not advisable to overtake at a road junction.

Positioning – page 135

1. Yes. The left lane is correct if you are going straight ahead at a roundabout with two approach lanes.
2. Yes. You should keep well to the left when turning right out of narrow side roads. This leaves room for vehicles turning in.
3. No. 3 should be closer to the kerb in order not to mislead other road users.
4. No. 4 is already over the centre line, thus blocking oncoming traffic.
5. Yes. Road E is a one-way street, because the Give Way lines go right across the road.
6. No. 6 is driving on the centre line, risking a head-on collision with a vehicle

doing the same coming the other way.
7. No. The rule is keep to the left, unless overtaking or turning right, 7 is doing neither of those.
8. No. 8 should have waited in road D for both sides to be clear. There is not enough room to wait in the gap in the central reservation.
9. Yes. 9 is correctly positioned to 10.
10. No. 11 should go around the back of the oncoming traffic.

Junctions – page 136

1. No. The compulsory Left Turn Ahead sign prohibits this.
2. No. The No Left Turn and No Entry signs prohibit this.
3. Yes. Because 3's exit into road C is clear.
4. No. The No U-turn sign prohibits this.
5. Yes. It is a compulsory left turn in the lane that 5 is in.
6. No. The sign Ahead Only prohibits turning left or right.
7. No. 6's exit into road D is blocked by traffic, so it may not enter the yellow box.
8. No. The sign No Vehicles prohibits this.
9. Yes. There is no sign to prohibit this.
10. No. The No Right Turn sign prohibits this.

Level Crossings – page 137

1. False. After the amber lights, red lights will flash,

then the barriers will come down.
2. True. Large means over 55 feet (16.8 metres) long or 6 feet 6 inches (2.9 metres) wide or 38 tonnes total weight. Slow means 5mph or less.
3. False. Get everybody out of the vehicle and phone the signalman. Only then try to move the vehicle.
4. True. An advance warning sign like this tells you there are no barriers.
5. True. The lights will go out and the barriers go up when it is safe to cross.
6. False. Never zigzag around the barriers. Phone the signalman for advice.
7. True. Never drive 'nose to tail' over crossings just in case the traffic stops ahead and you get stuck on the crossing.
8. True.
9. True.
10. True!

Motorway regulations – page 138

1. No. The flashing red lights mean you must not enter the slip road.
2. No.
3. Yes, motorcycles over 50cc are allowed.
4. No; U-turns are illegal on motorways.
5. No. The hard shoulder is for emergencies and breakdowns only. You may park only at a service area.
6. Yes. The sign indicates the right-hand lane is closed ahead.
7. Yes. The rule 'keep to the

left unless overtaking' applies to motorways as well as ordinary roads.
8 No.
9. No. LGVs are restricted to the left and middle lanes of a three-lane motorway.
10. No. You are not allowed to reverse on the motorway. If you miss your exit, you must go on to the next one.

Motorways – page 139

Right-hand lane closed 7
Acceleration lane 20
Main carriageway 5
Hard shoulder 9
Central reservation 10
Slip road 19
Deceleration lane 18
Advisory speed limit
50mph 6
Countdown markers 1
1 mile to exit 3
Leave at next exit 13
Half mile to next exit 2
Do not go further in
this lane 11
Exit number 4
Change lane 12
Red coloured studs 15
Green coloured studs 14
Amber coloured studs 16
White coloured studs 17
Compulsory speed limit
50mph 22
End of restriction 21

4. Your Vehicle

In this section we need to look at the car you are, or will be, driving. I need to discuss the kinds of administrative documents you must obtain, how to detect mechanical faults and defects, the use of safety equipment, loading, towing, fuel and pollution.

There is quite a lot of information to take in, but the Theory Test contains a number of questions on these topics so you need to know the answers. More importantly, the mechanical condition of your car can affect your safety, that of your passengers and that of everyone else who uses the road.

You are not expected to have detailed mechanical knowledge, but you should be able to detect the most common mechanical faults and defects that can affect safety. To this end there are a number of regulations you are required to obey that are designed to ensure your car meets minimum safety standards. These include your use of safety equipment, and the way you load your vehicle or use it for towing.

In addition, your car is required to meet exhaust emission standards in order to keep pollution to a minimum.

Because of the volume of things I must tell you about, you may need to refer to the pages that follow several times. To help you use this section for future reference, I have split the information into a number of topic areas. Where appropriate, specific details and facts are included that you will recognise from earlier sections of the book. The six topic areas concerned are:

- Administrative Documents, the Law and Traffic Regulations
- Safety Equipment
- Basic Car Care, Maintenance and Fault Spotting
- Automatics
- Safety Factors Relating to Your Vehicle; Loading and Towing
- Environmental Issues.

Administrative Documents, the Law and Traffic Regulations

If driving is about going places, following the law and traffic regulations is largely about going places safely. But before you can go anywhere, you will need to be in possession of certain vital documents.

If your vehicle is under three years old, there are four documents you must possess; if it is over three, then there are five. Some of this documentation – driving licence, insurance policy – is directly associated with you as an individual. The rest – registration document, tax disc and MOT certificate – is associated with your vehicle.

Driving licence

It is an offence to drive on the roads or permit another person to drive a motor vehicle without a current licence for the class of vehicle being driven.

If you are stopped by the police for any reason, they may request to see your driving licence. It's a good idea to carry it with you, but if you don't have it when you are stopped, you must take it to a police station of your choice within seven days.

You may drive a car as long as you hold – and have signed – either a provisional or a full licence issued in the UK, provided that if you are the holder of a provisional licence, you are

Carry your licence – if you're stopped by the police, they may want to see it.

accompanied and supervised by a person over 21 who has held a full licence for three years.

You may also drive if you have applied to renew a provisional or full licence, and you are not disqualified from doing so.

If you hold a visitors' or international permit issued abroad, it will be valid for up to one year from the date of your last entry into this country. Special conditions apply to new residents in the UK.

Registration document

All cars must be registered before being used on the road. A registration document – familiarly called a 'log book' – is issued together with a 'registration mark' for use on the number plates of the vehicle.

Alterations to the registered particulars must be notified to the Driver Vehicle Licensing Agency (DVLA) in Swansea. Alterations include a change of ownership, colour, engine size and change of use. The vehicle registration document contains details of the make and model of the vehicle, the year it was first registered and the engine size and number. Although the name and address of the registered owner, or keeper, is also shown, the document is not proof of ownership.

Excise licence

This is commonly referred to as the 'road tax', and the circular piece of paper you receive to show you have paid it as the 'tax disc'. All cars under 25 years old must be taxed if they are kept on the highway, even if they are never driven (certain disabled drivers are exempt).

Licences are valid for 6 or 12 months on payment of the appropriate fee, and you must renew the licence before it expires. When renewing you will have to produce a valid certificate of insurance (see item below) and a Vehicle Test Certificate (MOT) if your car is more than three years old.

The licence (tax disc) must be displayed on the windscreen so that its particulars are clearly visible.

Insurance

It is an offence to use a vehicle on the roads that is not properly insured for the purposes for which it is being used. The minimum requirements of the Road Traffic Act require that the following must be covered for 'third party' risks:

- Death and injury to others or damage to their property
- Emergency medical treatment.

In most cases you will want to take out insurance for more than these minimum requirements. The most common policies available are: third party, fire and theft (as above, plus fire damage to your vehicle and theft of your vehicle), and comprehensive (this is the most expensive and, as well as the above, includes damage to your own vehicle, replacement of parts damaged in an accident, and personal injury costs).

Be warned – if you drive a vehicle owned by someone else you may not be insured at all and unless they have made special provision any insurance will be minimum legal cover. You should check their policy before driving.

The cost of your insurance will vary from one insurance company to another. The younger you are the

The make of your car, its power and engine size will all affect the premium.

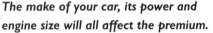

greater the cost is likely to be, because you will be considered a higher risk, although increasingly you will find insurance companies willing to give discounts to new drivers who take additional post-test training. The area where you live, how you intend to use your car, its make, power and engine size will all affect the premium. If you get any court convictions through driving misdemeanours, these can also significantly increase the cost.

Your insurance company will provide you with a detailed policy document containing full – and usually complex – details of the contract you have agreed. In addition, you will receive a short and simple document called an 'insurance certificate'.

This will normally state the dates of cover, who is insured, the type of vehicle and the level of insurance. You must produce this document when asked to do so by the police. You are allowed seven days to take it to a police station of your choice.

Vehicle Test Certificate

This is usually referred to as an MOT test certificate (MOT standing for Ministry of Transport). The MOT test is an annual check to see that your car complies with construction, use and lighting regulations. The test includes checking: braking system, steering, lighting, reflectors, tyres, indicators, washers, wipers, wheels, bodywork, suspension, horn, seat belts, and exhaust noise and emissions.

All cars over three years old must be tested at an approved centre once a year. You are allowed to have your vehicle tested up to one month before the current certificate expires. Your new certificate will still run for

one year from the date your old one expires.

It is an offence to use a motor vehicle, to which the regulations apply, without a current MOT test certificate – except to drive to an approved test centre where an appointment has been booked, or to take it away from the test station (where it failed its test), or to correct the faults on which it failed. As with your insurance details, you must show a current MOT certificate to the police within seven days of a request being made.

Production of documents

I have already explained that if requested to do so by the police, you must produce your driving licence, insurance or MOT certificate at a police station of your choice within seven days.

However, you will not commit an offence if you produce your documents after seven days, as long as you have a good reason. For example, you might be away from home for urgent personal reasons. If you lose any documents, you can always obtain a duplicate. You must inform the police station and will normally be granted extra time before a summons is issued.

The best bet is to make sure you keep your documents in a safe place.

Stopping regulations

So much for the documentation with which you must comply; there are also regulations to do with stopping that must be obeyed. You must stop:

- When directed to by a policeman or traffic warden
- At a school-crossing patrol showing a Stop–Children sign
- At stop lines accompanying a Stop sign
- At red, amber or red and amber traffic lights
- At pelican crossings when the light is red, or when flashing amber and pedestrians are still crossing
- At a zebra crossing to give way to pedestrians
- At flashing red lights on a motorway or at a level crossing
- If involved in an accident.

Conversely, you must not stop or park in any of the many places listed as examples in the *Highway Code*. They may seem a matter of common sense, but a walk or drive down any road should be enough to convince you that we are unlikely to learn them from the example of others! As a general rule you may not park or stop where:

- A road sign tells you not to wait
- It would cause danger to other road users
- It would make it difficult for others to see
- It would make the road narrow
- It would hold up traffic or cause inconvenience
- Emergency vehicles stop, enter or leave premises.

It is an offence to block access to premises housing emergency vehicles.

Driving offences

If you fail in your obligation to carry or possess the correct documents, don't stop when properly commanded or otherwise break any laws while driving, you will leave yourself open to a possible conviction. Certain offences involve automatic disqualification for a minimum period of one year, along with other possible penalties. They are:

■ Manslaughter by the driver of a motor vehicle
■ Causing death by dangerous driving
■ A second dangerous driving offence within three years
■ Racing on the highway
■ Driving under the influence of drink or drugs
■ Driving while disqualified.

Other offences may result in disqualification or licence endorsement at the discretion of the court. Under the penalty points system, accumulation of 12 points for endorsable offences within a three-year period will result in a minimum of six months disqualification. These points are endorsed on your licence. The number of points you are given for the offence is determined by Parliament according to the gravity of the act.

Fines are also settled by courts and three-quarters are imposed by fixed penalty, and in particular those for speeding and parking. You must contest the case in court or pay within 28 days, otherwise the fine increases by 50 per cent.

There is worse... The most serious offences may result in a prison sentence. The maximum length of any such sentence is determined by Parliament, but a court may impose some form of community service or probation instead.

I have brought the problem of driving while under the influence of alcohol to your attention at various points throughout this book. The problem is important enough to restate here. The only sensible advice is not to drink any alcohol at all if you intend to drive. It is an offence to drive a car, or be in charge of it, on a public road if the proportion of alcohol in your body is above the prescribed limits:

Sleeping off the effects of alcohol in a lay-by might seem sensible – but it's still an offence if you're over the limit.

- 35 microgrammes per 100 millilitres of breath
- 80 milligrammes per 100 millilitres of blood
- 107 milligrammes per 100 millilitres of urine.

The police have wide powers to stop cars. Once you have been stopped, if the police officer suspects you may have been drinking, or if you were involved in an accident or have committed a moving traffic violation, then you can be required to give a sample of breath. Refusal to supply a sample of breath is an offence, as is trying to but failing in the attempt – by, for example, not blowing long and hard enough. Refusal at the police station will result in a minimum 12-month driving ban.

Being in charge of a car while over the limit can also be an offence – for example, if you are parked in a lay-by 'sleeping it off'. If you are found to be over the limit, a 12-month ban is now the minimum penalty the courts can impose, and the maximum fine is £5,000.

Safety Equipment

Modern technology has enabled car manufacturers to provide cars with an ever-increasing array of safety features in even modestly-priced vehicles.

Some safety equipment, such as seat belts and certain lights, is required by law and also has regulations concerning its use. Other equipment, such as air bags and alarm systems, is optional but even so it will only afford maximum protection if used and serviced in accordance with the manufacturer's instructions.

In this section, I shall explain the legal requirements and touch briefly on optional extras.

Seat belts

The regulations regarding seat belts are a little complicated because they have changed several times since 1964. You really only need to know the basic requirements:

- All new cars are now built with front and rear seat belts
- Some older cars do not have rear seat belts
- If seat belts are fitted, the driver

and any adult passengers (14 years old and over) must wear them, whether sitting in the front or rear of the car

- Adult passengers – defined as aged 14 or over – are personally responsible for ensuring they wear a seat belt
- The driver is responsible for those passengers under 14 years of age
- Special rules apply to children. The table at the top of the facing page summarises the requirements. It is taken from *The Driving Manual* published by Driving Standards Agency (DSA) and Her Majesty's Stationery Office (HMSO).

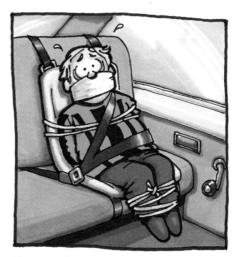

The term 'appropriate restraint' used in the table is defined as a child seat or harness suitable for the child's weight.

	Front Seat	Rear Seat	Responsibility?
Driver	Seat belt	—	Driver
Child under 1	Approved baby carrier suitable for the child's weight	Baby carrier with seat belt or carrycot restrained by straps	Driver
Child aged 1, 2 or 3	Appropriate restraint or seat belt	Appropriate restraint or booster seat used with seat belt	Driver
Child aged 4–13	Seat belt or appropriate restraint	Seat belt or appropriate restraint	Driver
Passengers 14+	Seat belt	Seat belt	Passenger

It is not illegal to carry more children in your car than there are seat belts available, but you should remember that you endanger their lives if you do so.

Regardless of the law, remember that seat belts can save your life. Remember also that in an accident a rear passenger not wearing a seat belt can be thrown forward and injure or kill a front passenger or the driver. Look after your seat belts, keep them clean and dry and check them periodically for any damage; they may be lifesavers – literally.

Head restraints

Head restraints are another safety feature of cars that can significantly reduce the severity of injury even in relatively minor accidents. Do note, however, that they can cause more harm than good if they're not adjusted properly. Always consult your manufacturer's handbook, but as a general rule the upper edge of the head restraint should be at approximately eye level and never at neck level.

Child locks

Many cars have special locks fitted to the rear doors. When carrying children in the back of the car you can set the locks so that the rear doors can only be opened from outside the car.

Electric windows

Children and electric windows do not always go well together and the combination can be dangerous. Many cars now have a device fitted which, when switched on, stops the windows being operated except from the driver's seat.

Car security

Nobody wants to have their car stolen or to have anything stolen from it. Unfortunately, car crime is an enormous problem for all of us.

Many modern cars come with built-in sophisticated anti-theft systems, while older vehicles can be fitted with such items as accessories. The best bet is probably to seek advice from your vehicle manufacturer as to the level of protection you can obtain within your budget. Don't forget, though, that common sense and a little care are just as important as any sophisticated device. If you leave your keys in your car or forget to lock it, expensive equipment won't help much.

Lighting regulations

Manufacturers ensure that the lights fitted to a vehicle comply with the regulations. But it is the driver's responsibility to ensure their vehicle lights remain in working order and comply with any new regulations that may come into force.

The following must be fitted:

- Two headlamps
- Two sidelamps
- Two rear lamps (tail lights)
- Number plate lamp
- Two red reflectors at the rear
- Flashing direction indicators (front and rear) (from 1965)
- Rear stop lamps (from 1971)
- Rear fog lamps (from 1980)

Headlamps

- Must be a white or yellow light to the front
- Must be permanently dipped or fitted with a dipping device
- Should be securely fitted and kept in a clean and efficient condition
- Must be switched off when the vehicle is stationary, except at

Many modern cars come with built-in sophisticated anti-theft systems.

Your headlights must be capable of being dipped in order not to dazzle oncoming drivers.

traffic lights, at Stop lines, in traffic and at junctions, etc
- Should be lit when driving after lighting-up time, unless street lights are less than 200 metres apart
- Must be used in poor daytime visibility.

Sidelamps
- Must show white to the front through frosted glass or other diffusing material
- May be incorporated in the headlamps provided they meet the height and width specifications.

Rear lamps (tail lights)
- Must show to the rear through red material.

Number plate lamp
- Must be a white light to illuminate the rear number plate.

Red rear reflectors
- Must be two showing to the rear
- May be combined with tail lights mounted vertically
- Circular types must be at least four centimetres in diameter. Other types must have a minimum reflective area equal to a four-centimetre circle.

Flashing direction indicators
- Are required to be fitted at the front and rear on all cars registered after 1965, and they should be amber in colour
- Should flash between 60 and 120 times a minute
- Must show through frosted glass or other diffusing material
- Must be kept clean and in efficient working order.

Stop lamps
- Are obligatory on cars first used on or after 1971
- Must display a steady, non-flashing red light when the foot brake is applied
- Failure of one bulb must not extinguish the other

■ Must be kept clean and working properly.

Rear fog lamps

■ Are obligatory on cars first used on or after April 1, 1980
■ If one lamp is fitted, it must be positioned on the offside of the car. If two are fitted, they must be symmetrical
■ They may only be used during adverse weather conditions where visibility is reduced to less than 100 metres.

Optional lighting

If fitted and wired, optional lighting must comply with regulations and be in working order. Examples are reversing lamps and front fog lamps.

Reversing lamps must show a white light. They are normally operated by a switch which is activated by the engagement of reverse gear. If they are operated by a manual switch, a warning light must indicate to the driver that they are switched on.

Fog lamps must be a symmetrically matched pair with either yellow or white beams, permanently deflected. They may only be used in fog or falling snow, unless they are fitted more than two feet from the ground.

Parking and hazard warning lights

A car must be parked with lights, except if it is:

■ Parked on a road with a speed limit of not more than 30mph
■ Parked further than 10 metres from any road junction
■ Parked close to and parallel to the kerb on the left-hand side of the road (except in a one-way street).

Hazard warning lights make all four indicators flash at the same time. You normally turn them on by pressing a switch marked with a triangle. The triangle flashes on and off when the hazard lights are in use to act as a warning and remind you to turn them off.

Only use hazard lights to warn other traffic when you have broken down or have had to stop in an emergency; never use them as an excuse to stop or park illegally. Only use hazard warning lights when you are actually stopped, although there are two important exceptions to this: you may use warning lights on a motorway or on an unrestricted dual carriageway if you are forced to slow down quickly because of a hazard ahead.

There is another way of warning

other road users that you may be a potential hazard, and that is the warning triangle. It is not compulsory to carry a warning triangle in your car while driving in the UK. However, you are strongly advised to do so. You normally use the triangle to warn other traffic you have broken down.

On a two-way road you should place the triangle at the side of the road at least 50 metres behind your vehicle. On a motorway or dual carriageway, place the triangle at least 150 metres behind your vehicle.

General regulations

Finally, there are two regulations regarding lighting which you must know. No vehicle shall show:

- A red light to the front
- Any other light to the rear than red; or a white light for reversing.

The main exceptions are:

- Internal illumination
- Number plate lamp
- Direction indicators.

If it's fitted and wired, optional lighting must comply with regulations and be in working order.

Basic Car Care, Maintenance and Fault Spotting

Learning how a car works is not everyone's cup of tea. However, you do not need to know very much in order to pass your test and then drive safely. Nevertheless, you want your future car to stay reliable and not break down. You will also want to stay legal, and most importantly you want to drive a safe vehicle.

To achieve all this you need to exercise a little common sense and to take in a basic understanding of how to maintain your vehicle in a safe condition. You need to be able to spot safety problems with your car before they get too serious or expensive to repair. In the next few pages I have outlined some of the main problems that can arise and how to spot them. Unless you are a DIY enthusiast you will probably take your car to a garage when service or repairs are needed.

To help you learn what you need I have divided the topic into the sub-sections listed here:

■ Regular safety checks
■ Tyres

■ Braking system
■ Steering system
■ Engine temperature gauge
■ Oil pressure gauge
■ Ignition warning light
■ Ignition system
■ Transmission system
■ Engine.

Regular recommended safety checks

The *Highway Code*, The Driving Standards Agency book, *The Driving Manual*, and leading motoring organisations all recommend the safety checks listed below. On a daily basis you should check:

■ **Tyres** – walk around the car and check for obvious faults, such as a flat tyre
■ **Lights and indicators** – check they are all in working order, and clean
■ **Windscreen and windows** – clean them whenever necessary
■ **Windscreen washer bottle** – keep it topped up with water and cleaning fluid
■ **Brakes** – as soon as possible after

moving off check that your brakes are working properly

- **Secure loads and equipment** – check that everything carried is secure (for example: roof-rack, luggage, spare wheel, tools).

The next list is recommended regular safety checks. For many checks 'regular' means checking at the intervals as recommended in your car's handbook. In all other cases it is safest to think of regular as meaning at least once a week:

- **Engine oil** – check the engine oil when the car is on level ground and the engine is cold, and top up as necessary

Only check the radiator when it is cool.

- **Radiator** (if there is one) – check water level and top up as necessary
- **Tyres** – check they are sound and at the right pressures
- **Brakes** – check the fluid in the brake fluid reservoir
- **Steering** – check for excessive free play of the steering wheel. If in doubt, consult a qualified garage mechanic
- **Windscreen wipers** – check condition of blades and arms, and ensure they are working properly
- **Seat belts** – check they are easily operated
- **Exhaust** – repair or replace a defective system immediately
- **Horn** – check it works.

The above checks should be carried out in addition to regular service checks. The car handbook will state the recommended intervals between services.

The tyres

The tyres on your car are the only part of the vehicle in contact with the road. This area of contact is small, little more than the size of the sole of your shoe for each tyre. Tyres that are in poor condition cannot do their job properly. They must be treated with care, and checked, maintained and replaced when necessary.

There are two basic types of tyre in use: cross-ply and radial-ply. The main difference between the two is in the way they are made. The body of either type of tyre is made up of layers of cord which is sometimes covered with steel mesh. The outside part of the tyre is made of a thick layer of rubber or a rubber synthetics mixture.

In cross-ply tyres the cords are arranged so that they cross each other diagonally, forming a grid.

Cross-ply tyres:

■ Are generally cheaper
■ Have a shorter life
■ Have thicker walls
■ Are less flexible
■ Have poorer grip
■ Distort more when cornering and when less of the tread is in contact with the road.

By contrast, radial-ply tyres have the cords running at right-angles across the tyres, making the walls of the tyre thinner and more flexible.

Radial-ply tyres:

■ Are generally more expensive
■ Have a longer life
■ Have softer, thinner walls
■ Are more flexible
■ Have better grip
■ Have flexible walls, allowing more even road contact when cornering.

Because radial- and cross-ply tyres have different cornering and braking characteristics, it is advisable to keep the same type of tyre on all four wheels of your car. Most modern cars are fitted with

You can't check tyre pressures just by looking at them.

radial-ply tyres because of their advantages (outlined above), but many cross-ply tyres are available, so take care to fit the right type. If you are going to mix radial and cross-ply tyres, the following legal rules apply:

- Never put radial- and cross-ply on the same axle
- Never put radials on the front and cross-ply on the rear.

There are other minimum legal requirements for tyres, and the law is very strict about them. It is an offence to use tyres that are:

- An incorrect type or size for the car
- Wrongly inflated (incorrect pressure)
- Cut or bulging
- Showing tyre cords
- Worn below the minimum tread depth. The minimum legal requirement for cars, vans, trailers and caravans is not less than 1.6mm tread depth across the central three-quarters of the breadth of the tyre and around the entire outer circumference.

The only way you can be sure that your tyres are in good condition is to check them regularly. On a daily basis you should carry out a visual check for any obvious faults. Every week you should look specifically for:

- **Cuts and bulges** – look at the tyre walls, not forgetting those facing under the car
- **Stone, glass, etc**. – caught in the treads, these can damage or puncture the tyre and should be removed
- **Oil and grease** – reduces grip if left on the tyres. Clean off using water and a little mild detergent
- **Adequate tread depth** – a visual check may not be sufficient; if in doubt, use a gauge or consult a tyre expert
- **Uneven tread wear** – this may be due to a mechanical defect, such as:
  - wheels not aligned properly perhaps because of hitting the kerb
  - wheels out of balance
  - suspension fault
  - brake fault
  - incorrect air pressures

Correct tyre pressures

You cannot check tyre pressures just by looking. You must find out from the car handbook what the recommended pressures for front and rear tyres are in various conditions. Then use a reliable pressure gauge to check the pressures. Bear in mind that pressure readings will not be accurate unless the tyre is cold, which really means that it hasn't been driven a lot before taking the reading. This is because air pressure increases as the temperature rises, and as the tyres roll over the road surface, the friction warms the air inside. The car manufacturer's recommended pressures always assume that a tyre is cold when checked.

Too much pressure in a tyre gives a bumpy ride and light steering, causes tyres to wear in the centre of the tread, and reduces grip because there is less tread in contact with the road.

Too little pressure makes the steering feel heavier and makes the car less stable on bends because the tyre walls flex too much and overheat.

It's best to follow this general rule: pressures should be higher for a car carrying a heavy load, or for long distance journeys at high speed. But always look in your car handbook for the recommended pressures.

However carefully you drive, your tyres will eventually wear out. Paying attention to the points below will extend their life and reduce the risk of unnecessary damage:

- Keep air pressures correct
- Avoid pot-holes whenever it is safe to do so, and slow down on temporary road surfaces
- Don't scrape or drive over kerbs

With low pressure, the tyre walls flex too much and overheat, making the car unstable on bends.

■ Avoid high speeds and hard cornering, which cause extra wear
■ Braking causes most wear, so avoid braking too hard
■ Fierce acceleration causes considerable wear.

The braking system

Brakes provide the means by which you can slow down or stop your car under control. They also prevent the car moving when parked.

The braking system must have two means of operation, or consist of two systems with separate operation, and if one system fails, the other must be sufficient to stop the car safely. The systems must also work when the engine is not running. There are two main types of braking system: drum brakes and disc brakes.

A drum brake normally consists of a brake drum which rotates with the road wheel, and two brake shoes with friction linings. When the brakes are applied the shoes are forced outwards to grip the inside of the brake drum.

Disc brakes are similar in principle to a bicycle braking system. Steel-backed pads of friction material are applied to both sides of a disc to slow it down. Disc brakes have several advantages over drum brakes. Their friction surfaces are in open contact with the air, which reduces the risk of overheating, they normally adjust automatically and they are easier to inspect and maintain.

When you depress the brake pedal, it forces a piston forward in the hydraulic master cylinder. This forces the brake fluid through the closed system, which in turn creates pressure to push the brake shoe (or pad) onto the rotating wheel drum (or disc), and so slows down the car.

Like anything else mechanical, brakes are subject to defects in operation. It is important that you can detect faults with the brakes quickly, and know what remedial action to take. Here are the most typical faults:

■ The car pulls to one side when you brake – your brakes may be incorrectly adjusted. You should seek assistance from a qualified mechanic
■ You press the brake pedal and it feels 'spongy' – this may mean that there is air in the system. Seek assistance urgently
■ Your brakes no longer seem efficient – they may require adjusting, the pads may need replacing or there may be a leak in the hydraulic system. Seek assistance urgently. A similar lack

of efficiency may be caused by the brakes becoming overheated. This 'brake fade' can occur with prolonged use

- Your brake warning light comes on – either the pads may be worn or the brake fluid may be low, or there may be a system fault. You should seek assistance urgently
- The hand brake does not hold your car still on a hill – it needs adjusting, or the cable may need replacing.

The steering system

The steering wheel enables you to pivot the vehicle's front wheels to the left or the right and, by doing so, steer the car. There are two main types of steering system: steering box, and rack and pinion. Most modern cars are fitted with rack and pinion, which is

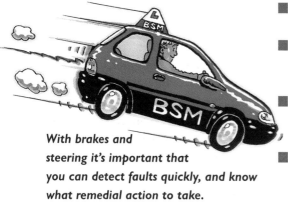

With brakes and steering it's important that you can detect faults quickly, and know what remedial action to take.

simpler in design and needs less maintenance than the steering box.

A greater number of cars than used to be the case are now equipped with power-assisted steering. This makes steering easier and makes the steering feel light, particularly at very low speeds. However, it also makes it much easier to turn the wheels while stationary, and this should be avoided in order to prevent unnecessary wear to the tyres (and that applies to non-power-assisted steering as well). Steering is crucial to your safety. Repairs or adjustments should only be carried out by a qualified person. If you think that there is something wrong with the steering system, seek expert advice as soon as possible. The common faults to look out for are:

- Excess free play of the steering wheel
- Sudden heavy or erratic steering means you may have a puncture
- Sustained heavy steering may be possible failure of power-assisted steering, where fitted
- Uneven wear of the tyres may indicate that the steering needs adjustment
- Vibration in steering at specific speeds may mean the front wheels need balancing.

Engine temperature gauge

An internal combustion engine produces mechanical power from controlled explosions inside the engine cylinders. Heat is generated in the cylinders and an efficient cooling system is needed to absorb this heat and keep the engine at its operating temperature. Most engines are cooled by water, which is pumped through special channels around the engine.

The temperature gauge shows you whether the system is operating within its normal temperature range. If excessive temperature is recorded you should stop driving.

There are several reasons for excessive engine temperature – not least being hot summer days – but here are the common causes:

■ **A broken fan belt** – the fan belt normally operates the water pump and radiator fan
■ **A lack of water** – a broken hose or a leaking radiator can easily cause loss of water and leave insufficient to do its job
■ **A blocked radiator** – most commonly caused by ice. An anti-freeze solution should be used in cold conditions to prevent the water from freezing.

Oil pressure gauge/ warning light

Oil is needed to lubricate the moving parts of an engine and to help carry heat away from critical parts. Oil is forced, under high pressure, along a series of pipes and channels to all moving parts.

If there is a fall in the oil pressure, the oil pressure gauge and/or the oil warning light will warn you. If this should happen, stop as soon as possible and switch off the engine. If you cannot rectify the fault – you may just have run low on oil – seek expert advice, but do not drive any further.

Other than a lack of oil, a drop in oil pressure may be caused by:

■ Burst oil pipes
■ Broken oil pump
■ A very worn engine.

You may notice that your oil warning light flickers on intermittently, perhaps particularly as you drive round bends. This is likely to mean a low level of oil in the sump. As you steer, what little oil there is washes from one side of the sump to the other causing the oil warning light to operate. You should stop and check the oil level using the dipstick provided on the engine block of your car. When you check the oil, make sure your car is on level ground – if you are parked on a slope you will get a false reading.

Ignition warning light

The ignition warning light should come on when the engine's electrical circuits are switched on – always check that it does. When you activate the starter motor and start the engine, the alternator should begin to generate electricity and the ignition light should go out.

If the engine tick-over (idling) speed is low, the ignition light may not go out until you depress the accelerator slightly. If the light still remains on, there is a fault. Switch off the engine.

Loose electrical wires or connections are a common fault.

If the light comes on while you are driving, you should stop as soon as possible, switch off the engine and rectify the fault.

Loose electrical wires or connections are a common fault, and so are burnt out brushes in the alternator. The alternator is usually operated by the fan belt. If the fan belt breaks, the alternator will cease to provide the electricity needed to run the engine and other equipment, and the battery will gradually lose its power (that is, go flat).

The ignition system

The ignition system provides the electric sparks that are needed to ignite the fuel-and-air mixture in the cylinders of the engine. A low-tension voltage from the battery is converted into high-tension voltage by the coil or electronic ignition. This voltage is transmitted through the high-tension lead from the coil to the distributor cap. As the engine rotates, the rotor arm inside the distributor completes a sequence of contacts to the spark plugs. The spark plugs provide a fixed gap in the combustion chamber of the engine across which the high voltage spark can arc. This spark ignites the fuel-and-air mixture in the combustion chamber. Common faults are:

- Blown fuse
- Flat battery
- Loose battery terminals
- Worn, dirty or incorrectly adjusted contact breaker points or spark plugs
- Worn rotor arm
- Faulty leads.

The transmission system

The car's engine provides the power to turn the wheels, but somehow that power has to get to the wheels, and that's the purpose of the transmission system. In non-automatic cars the system consists of:

- The clutch
- The gearbox
- The final drive (the 'differential').

The clutch provides the link between the engine and the gearbox. It makes it possible to disconnect the

The spark generated by the spark plug ignites the fuel-and-air mixture.

transmission from the engine in order to change the gears smoothly. It allows you to progressively engage the drive of the engine to the road wheels so that you can move off smoothly, and then leave the engine running ('idling') when the car is temporarily at a stop, say at traffic lights.

The gearbox enables you to match the power of the engine to both the speed of the car and the amount of power needed to keep it moving.

The final drive, or 'differential' as it is often called, enables the inside wheel to turn slower than the outer wheel when you steer around a curve.

The transmission system should require little or no attention between your regular car service periods. Any faults are best rectified by a qualified mechanic.

The engine

You are not required to have detailed knowledge of a car engine in order to pass your Theory Test. However, your engine will only do its job efficiently and remain in good working order if you look after it. This means not just careful servicing and maintenance but also sensible driving.

For your information, a very brief explanation of how an engine works is given below, followed by a few typical simple faults that you may be able to rectify without great difficulty.

The engine system can be broken down into six functions:

■ The mechanical system is the main body of the engine made up of all the parts inside and attached to the cylinder block

■ The lubrication system supplies oil to lubricate the moving parts of the engine

■ The fuel system feeds a petrol-air mixture to the engine's cylinders which, when ignited, provides the power to make the car move

■ The ignition system was described earlier

■ The cooling system removes excess heat from the engine

■ The exhaust system removes burnt and used fuel from the engine.

Most cars are powered by a four-cylinder engine. Each cylinder is set in the engine block, which is usually made of cast iron. Pistons are forced up and down inside the cylinders, in a set sequence as follows:

1. Induction stroke
2. Compression stroke
3. Ignition stroke
4. Exhaust stroke

A system of valves controls the flow of air and fuel mixture into the cylinders, and the flow of burnt exhaust gases out of the cylinders. In the induction stroke, the piston travels down the cylinder drawing in a mixture of petrol and air from the carburettor through the open inlet valve. When the piston reaches the bottom of its stroke the inlet valve closes.

During the compression stroke both valves are closed and the piston is forced back up the cylinder, compressing the air-petrol mixture.

In the ignition stroke (sometimes called the power stroke), the spark from the sparking plug ignites the mixture. The burning gases expand causing the piston to be driven downwards, which produces engine power.

After this the exhaust valve opens, allowing gases to be forced out by the upward movement of the piston – the exhaust stroke. The exhaust valve closes and the cycle begins again.

The crankshaft converts the power into a rotary motion, which in turn creates the motion needed to turn the wheels. One complete cycle of the four strokes turns the crankshaft once.

Here are some common faults which you should be able to rectify yourself once you understand the basic workings of the engine:

- The engine misfires or will not run – this is likely to be an electrical fault or a fuel problem. It is worth checking for loose connections
- The engine will not start – you may be out of fuel, or the electrical circuits may be damp. You can check your fuel gauge and use an anti-damp spray

The engine may not start if the electrical circuits have become damp.

- The starter motor will not operate – your battery is probably flat. You can change the battery, use jump leads from another car or, in a manual car, you can push-start it with a little help from your friends
- The starter or solenoid clicks – the starter motor is probably jammed. You may need a new one. You can sometimes solve the problem by rocking your car backwards and forwards in gear with the ignition off. Some starter motors have a square end which can be turned with a spanner to release the mechanism
- A squealing noise from the engine area – the fan belt or alternator belt is probably slipping. You can adjust or replace
- Overheating – the fan belt may have snapped (as mentioned earlier) or a water hose may be leaking. A fuse could have blown on the electric cooling fan. You can replace the belt, hose or fuse.

You may, of course, put your car in the garage for even the most minor repair and do nothing but the basic safety checks yourself. Even so, you should find it useful to have some idea of what the problem may be. A little knowledge will help you understand your mechanic's explanations of necessary repairs.

If the fan belt snaps, emergency repairs can be effected with whatever tough, stretchable material may be to hand.

Automatics

Cars fitted with automatic transmission are becoming more popular. They simplify the task of driving by removing the need to make decisions continually about changing gear, and reducing the physical movements required to do so. When you drive an automatic car you should have more time to focus your attention on what is happening on the road around you.

If you pass your practical driving test in a car with automatic transmission your licence will not entitle you to drive a car with a manual gearbox. If you later wish to drive a manual, you will need to take another test. However, if you pass your test in a manual car you are also entitled to drive an automatic, and for this reason you are expected to have a basic understanding of automatics before you take your Theory Test.

To drive an automatic car safely, it is essential that you understand the different ways in which the controls operate and how to use them effectively. There are many variations of the controls, and you should always read the car's handbook before driving a particular make or model for the first time.

Correct use of automatic controls

A car with automatic transmission has no clutch pedal. It has a gearbox that not only senses the need for changes to higher or lower gears, but makes the necessary changes without actions by the driver.

In general, an automatic transmission changes to a higher gear as you increase speed and to a lower gear as you decrease speed. It also takes into account the load on the engine: for example, it will change down, if necessary, as you go uphill. There are occasions – for example, when driving down a long, steep hill – when you need a low gear, even though your speed is constant and the engine load is light. In this instance, the automatic transmission may not select the correct gear, and extra controls are fitted to allow for this.

Most automatics have a small selector lever which can be moved to one of five or more positions:

- **N** = Neutral – the engine can be started in this position
- **P** = Park – this position locks the transmission mechanically, and

should be used when parked. You must only select this position when the car is stationary with the engine stopped. It is possible to start the engine with the lever in this position

■ **R** = Reverse – this position allows you to drive backwards

■ **D** = Drive – this position is used to cause the car to go forward

■ **D1 & D2** – two drive positions. The D position is sometimes replaced by two drive positions, often marked D1 and D2. On some three-speed transmissions, D2 cuts out first gear when moving off. This allows a gradual and smooth pull-away, and is particularly useful in slippery conditions

■ **L** = Lock up or Hold – this position enables you to either select a lower gear or keep in (hold) a low gear. Examples of where you should use this position are:

- in heavy, slow traffic to avoid unnecessary upward and downward automatic gear changes
- before you start to drive down a long, steep hill.

Having started the engine with the selector at N or P, you select D, release the brakes and press the accelerator and the car will move forward. It will continue to do so, changing gears as necessary, as long as you apply sufficient pressure to the

In general with automatics, only use your right foot for the gas and brake pedals. The car can become unstable if you're braking and accelerating at the same time.

accelerator. Heavy acceleration will delay upward gear changes while the car builds up speed. The reason for this is that heavy acceleration on a level road can put much the same load on the engine as climbing a steep hill.

Other controls

Many automatics are fitted with the 'kick-down' control. It is operated by your foot pressing down sharply on the accelerator pedal, past the fully open position. This action overrides the automatic gear selection, and causes a quick change down to the next lower gear. You use it in situations where you need rapid acceleration, such as when overtaking. When you ease the pressure off the accelerator pedal, the transmission will return to the next higher gear.

Operation of foot controls

In normal driving, you should use your right foot to operate both the accelerator and brake pedals because:

■ It aids anticipation – you are forced into moving your foot off the accelerator to reach the brake if a situation develops where you may need to slow down

■ It prevents you from braking and accelerating at the same time, which makes the vehicle unstable and wears the car's systems.

There is one time when it is safe to use both feet, one on the brake, the other on the accelerator and that is when manoeuvring at slow speeds.

The hand brake

You should apply the hand brake whenever you are stationary. This is even more important when you are driving an automatic than when driving a car with a manual gearbox. If the selector lever is at D, L or R (or any equivalent position), a car fitted with automatic transmission will move off if you press the accelerator – even if this was accidental – unless the brakes are already applied. If the choke is in use, the engine speed will be higher, and even light pressure on the accelerator can cause the car to move off.

When the tick-over or slow-running speed of the engine is sufficient to start the car moving forward – described as 'creep' – the hand brake is necessary to keep it stationary. You should check any excessive creep, and have the tick-over adjusted if necessary. Drivers sometimes like to rely on creep to hold their car stationary when facing uphill, but it's very unwise. Use the hand brake for this – if the engine stopped for any reason, the car would roll backwards and you could have an accident.

Accelerator

The accelerator has a more direct effect in a car with automatic transmission, and is consequently very sensitive. You should take care to check that the engine idling speed is not too high, as this can cause the engine to keep driving the car even when no pressure is applied to the accelerator. In slow-moving traffic conditions, controlling creep with the foot brake is normal; but you don't want the creep effect exaggerated by a too high tick-over speed.

General driving tips

Because of their differences in operation, there are a few things you should bear in mind when switching from a manual- to an automatic-transmission vehicle. In an automatic, if you reduce pressure on the accelerator as you approach a junction or bend, this may cause the automatic transmission to select a

higher gear. For this reason, you must:

- Slow down before the bend or junction
- Accelerate gently as you turn into the bend or junction
- Use L (lock up) where necessary to negotiate sharp bends or steep, downhill junctions.

With a manual gearbox you can expect the engine to help brake the car. In general, the braking effect on automatics is usually less than it is with manual transmissions. The extent to which the engine will help slow down a car with automatic transmission will vary according to the selector position which is in use.

This completes the subject of automatics. You may wish to bear in mind that not only can automatics make driving more convenient – particularly in congested traffic – but they also offer help to physically disabled drivers. There are fewer tasks to perform with the hands and feet and, together with the many adaptations that can be fitted, this enables most physical disabilities to be overcome sufficiently to be able to drive safely.

Safety Factors Relating to Your Vehicle; Loading and Towing

Since you are still looking forward to the day when you pass your driving test and become a qualified driver, the notion that one day you might tow a trailer or caravan may not yet have entered your head.

Nevertheless, caravanning and camping are activities which are pursued by an increasing proportion of the population. At the bottom end of the scale you may need to fit a roof-rack to your car in order to create enough space to transport all your luggage and other equipment. Alternatively you may tow your own caravan or trailer tent.

Such activities can be enjoyable as well as economical and in order to ensure you are able to follow a few basic principles to keep you safe, you may be asked questions on these topics in the Theory Test.

This section provides you with the information you need to answer such questions. It can also be referred to in years to come when you may decide to engage in such activities.

For your convenience, I have divided this topic into two sections: roof-racks and heavy loads; towing a trailer or caravan.

Roof-racks and heavy loads

For safety reasons – and to avoid damaging the roof of your car – you

should always consult your car handbook or seek advice from an authorised dealer before fitting a roof-rack. You need to select one that is recommended for your model and make of car. Here are some important points to bear in mind:

■ There will be increased air resistance due to the weight of your roof-rack or ski-holders, and this can increase fuel consumption by over 13.6 litres (three gallons) per 1,000 miles. For this reason, remove them when they are not needed

■ Always ensure that the roof-rack is secured by following the fitting instructions carefully

■ Take extra care to ensure that any items you load onto the roof-rack are securely tied or held down and will not shift position when you corner or drive at high speed

■ A roof-rack or other heavy load – including extra passengers – will cause your car to handle quite differently than when it is lightly loaded. You will notice this particularly when driving around bends, so take extra care

■ You may need to increase your tyre pressures to cope with the extra load. Consult your car handbook

■ Heavy loads can also affect the angle of your headlamp beams. In some new cars a headlamp-range adjustment switch is available. When your headlamps are on dipped beam, adjust the headlamp range to suit your load. Such a

Over-heavy loading either at the front or back can make towing dangerous.

switch might have the following settings:

- **0** = Driver's seat occupied
- **1** = All seats occupied
- **2** = All seats occupied and load in the luggage compartment
- **3** = Driver's seat occupied and load in the luggage compartment

■ If an article should fall from your roof-rack take great care when attempting to retrieve it. If you cannot do so on a two-way road, advise the police at once and, if possible, warn other traffic. You should never attempt to retrieve the article from the carriageway of a motorway. Use the nearest emergency telephone to advise the police, and stay with your car.

Towing a trailer or caravan*

Installation of towing equipment is not a simple process, and I strongly recommend that you seek professional advice. If at all possible

* From July 1, 1996 new regulations apply to cars towing large trailers or caravans. Unless you have passed your test before that date you may be required to take an extra practical driving test. You should check with the DVLA, Swansea if you are unsure of your entitlement.

Take extra care to ensure that any items you load onto the roof-rack are securely tied or held down.

have any such equipment fitted by an authorised dealer for your make of car. They will have details of the permissible caravan or trailer load for your vehicle; and they will be in possession of specifications concerning installation, as well as any necessary modifications that you may need to make to your car's cooling system.

Permissible caravan and trailer loads must not be exceeded by the weight of the caravan or trailer:

■ The lower the weight of your load in relation to the weight of your car, the safer the combination will be

■ Ideally, the total weight of the loaded caravan or trailer should not be more than 85 per cent of the weight of your car when empty

■ And, in any case, whatever you are towing should never weigh more than your empty car

■ You will join your caravan or trailer to your car by means of a coupling ball and socket. The load exerted on these must not exceed or drop below specified values. This load is affected by the weight distribution achieved when you load your caravan or trailer. The best bet is to seek professional advice.

The overall stability of both the towing car and the caravan depends on your correctly distributing the weight of what is carried. As a general guide:

■ Light items and bulky goods – such as bedding – can be spread about to achieve a suitable 'nose weight' at the towing coupling

■ Load heavy items in a caravan or trailer over the axles and as near to the ground as possible

■ You can obtain a gauge from caravan accessory shops and dealers to check that the 'nose weight' is correct.

If you fit a good stabiliser to the tow-bar, you are likely to find it easier and safer to control your car and the caravan or trailer you are towing. A stabiliser will not cure incorrect loading problems or instability caused by a poor combination of a car and trailer or caravan. You will achieve greater stability in cross-winds and also when you are overtaken by large goods vehicles on the motorway.

Your caravan or trailer is also likely to prevent you seeing what is behind you through your normal driving mirrors. You will need to fit exterior towing mirrors so that you can see clearly along both sides of the caravan or trailer.

Fitting a stabiliser can make life easier in the slipstream of overtaking lorries.

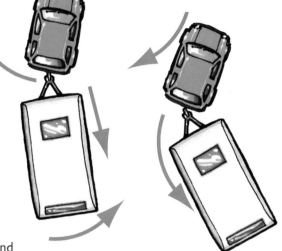

To reverse a caravan or trailer around a corner, you need to start by reversing the car in the opposite direction to the corner being reversed around.

Before you set out on a journey

All the normal safety checks and precautions you should take when setting out in your car apply with even greater force if you intend to tow a trailer or caravan.

In addition, you will need to consider your own experience and ability, and carry out specific checks to ensure your combination of car and caravan or trailer is safe to drive.

If you have no experience of towing you are strongly advised to attend a training course which covers aspects such as loading, manoeuvring and driving techniques. Your local British School of Motoring branch will be able to offer you help or put you in touch with one of the large caravanning organisations.

Learning to manoeuvre and reverse a caravan or trailer is not difficult but it does require practice. If possible, find somewhere quiet – like a car park off the public road – where you can practise and master the techniques involved.

Before you drive off, always check that your caravan or trailer:

- Is loaded correctly
- Has the correct pressure on the towbar
- Is correctly hitched up and that the hitch is fully locked on

The combination's increased length requires extra care when cornering.

- Has the breakaway cable correctly connected (if it is fitted with one)
- Has lights and indicators that are working correctly
- Has a jockey wheel and assembly that is fully retracted and stowed away correctly
- Has correctly functioning brakes
- Windows, doors and sky light are closed
- Has had its tyre pressures checked, and that they show no signs of uneven wear or cracking
- Has had its fuel supplies, such as liquid gas containers, switched off.

The law and towing

Speed limits are different when you are towing. They are:

- 30mph in built-up areas
- 50mph on single carriageway roads
- 60mph on motorways and dual carriageways.

On motorways with three or more lanes you are not allowed to tow a caravan or trailer in the outside lane unless the other lanes are closed.

You must not allow any passengers to travel in the caravan when it is being towed.

Driving tips when towing

Tyres – you may need to increase the tyre pressures of your car when towing a caravan or trailer. Consult your manufacturer's handbook about this.

Cornering – make sure that you have enough room when cornering and avoid sudden changes of direction. Be aware of the increased weight, length and width of your combined vehicles. The overall length of your combination is likely to be about twice the length of an average family car and will particularly affect the space you need when turning at junctions.

Braking and stopping – the extra weight means you need to brake earlier and as gently as possible. You should allow three times your normal stopping distance.

Overtaking – this will take much longer because of the extra weight. Be particularly careful not to cut back in after overtaking; be aware of the extra length you are towing behind you.

Snaking – your caravan or trailer may start to sway or swerve from side to side. If this happens:

- Ease off the gas slowly
- Allow for a certain amount of 'twitch' in the steering
- Reduce speed until the snaking stops

- Do not attempt to cure the problem by steering or braking hard. This is likely to make matters worse.

High-sided vehicles – when you pass or are overtaken by a high-sided vehicle, air turbulence can cause snaking. You need to take extra care and allow as much space as possible to reduce the effects of this.

Bad weather – reduce speed in high winds or cross-winds and avoid driving along exposed roads whenever possible.

As you can see, much of the advice in this topic of the loading and towing is common sense, and the rules and regulations are simply there to keep you safe.

Brake earlier and more gently when towing – you don't want the extra weight of the caravan or trailer catching you up unexpectedly.

Environmental Issues

Public concern has been growing about the effects of pollution on the environment in which we all live. While we recognise that motor vehicles are a necessary part of modern living we are increasingly aware of their damaging environmental consequences.

Nevertheless, a number of ways in which the problems can be contained or even reduced have been identified and these are the issues I will now explain. In general terms they fall under three areas of responsibility and action: government intervention; motor manufacturer research and development; individual actions of drivers.

Government intervention

Government policy clearly has an effect on how both passengers and goods are moved from place to place. Reductions in the level of service of public transport, together with a decline in the use of railways to transport freight, have contributed to the increased number of vehicles on our roads.

An increase in vehicular traffic will follow with a corresponding increase in damage to the environment. Points to consider are that:

1. Bigger and wider roads create changes to the landscape
2. Wildlife can be disturbed or destroyed
3. Stone buildings are slowly eroded by the exhaust fumes
4. The heavy volume of traffic weakens bridges and often weakens the structure of old buildings
5. Air pollution increases, particularly in towns with traffic congestion
6. Noise pollution can cause significant disruption near major roads or motorways.

The Government has acted in various ways:

- **MOT tests** – these have been extended to include a strict exhaust emission test. The test ensures that the engine is correctly tuned so that it will operate more efficiently. A more efficient engine uses less fuel and creates less air pollution
- **Unleaded petrol** – all new cars

with petrol engines must now be designed to run on unleaded petrol. When leaded petrol is used as fuel, significant quantities of lead escape through the exhaust and into the air

■ **Catalytic converters** – all new vehicles with petrol engines must now be fitted with catalytic converters. Carbon monoxide, nitrogen oxide and hydrocarbon emissions from the exhaust are reduced by up to 90 per cent

■ **Traffic management** – the Government is conducting a continuous programme of research into new ways of easing traffic flow. This research is not simply intended to speed up your journey. Traffic jams and slow-moving traffic increase air pollution levels. By keeping the traffic moving, the problem is eased

■ **Strict parking rules** – in major urban areas these aid traffic flow

■ **'Red routes'** – in London, for example, these cut journey times

■ **Light Rapid Transit systems (LRT)** – trams or 'metros' are being introduced in some towns and cities. They generally use electric power, which is more 'environmentally friendly' than petrol. They also provide an efficient form of public transport and encourage people to leave their cars at home.

The motor manufacturer

The primary purpose of all motor manufacturers is to make cars and other vehicles and then sell them to customers. Just like manufacturers of other goods, what they make and

Cars and other vehicles have a detrimental effect on our wildlife.

how they make it is partly dependent on what consumers are prepared to purchase. A mixture of government legislation and changing consumer priorities has led to a great deal of research both into how to make vehicles safe and how to make them more environmentally friendly.

Seat belts, side impact bars, air bags, collapsible steering columns, and other more complex features of vehicle design, have made our cars safer to drive. The aerodynamic bodies of cars and their more efficient engines use less fuel and therefore create less pollution, as does the introduction of unleaded fuel and catalytic converters.

Individual actions of drivers

There are a number of simple ways in which you personally can help to protect the environment by the choices you make about car ownership and driving. I shall summarise the main suggestions and advice given by the Department of Transport, the Driving Standards Agency and leading motor manufacturers.

Your car creates most pollution and uses most fuel for short journeys, especially when the engine is cold. Walk, cycle or use public transport whenever this is safe and practical.

When you buy a new car, make its fuel efficiency a high priority in your choice. The less petrol you burn, the less pollution you create.

Keep your car in good condition and have it serviced regularly. A car in good condition works more efficiently and therefore uses less fuel and emits less harmful gases.

Check your tyre pressures regularly and ensure the tyres are at the correct pressure. Under-inflated tyres cause your car to use more fuel.

Use unleaded fuel. If you have purchased an older car, which only runs on leaded petrol, consider having the engine converted. This can be achieved on most models, so consult your dealer or garage.

Remove any unnecessary goods or luggage from your car when you don't need them, as extra weight uses extra fuel.

If possible, remove your roof-rack – if you have one fitted – when you don't need it. It affects the aerodynamics of your car and uses more fuel.

Take care with toxic waste. Take oil waste, old batteries and used tyres to a garage or a local authority tip where they can be recycled or disposed of safely, as they can cause pollution if disposed of incorrectly.

Never pour used oil down the drain or into the ground. This is illegal and you could be prosecuted.

Adopt a sensible driving style. This will help you to keep the exhaust emissions within reasonable limits and reduce noise pollution.

Only use your horn when you need to warn others of your presence. It is illegal to sound your horn in a built-up area between 11:30pm and 7am.

Try to plan ahead and avoid harsh braking – one of the biggest wasters of fuel.

Accelerate as gently as possible in normal conditions. Unnecessarily harsh acceleration increases fuel consumption considerably. 'Jackrabbit' starts, with screeching tyres and high engine speeds, increase the noise level by up to 18 decibels.

Use your gears correctly and avoid over-revving the engine in a low gear.

Think about your speed and consider slowing down.

Driving at 70mph uses up to 30 per cent more fuel than driving at 50mph.

Just as we have to share the roads with others, we also have to share the environment in which we live. In one form or another pollution affects everybody, and anything we can do as individuals to keep this problem to a minimum will be of benefit to society.

'Jackrabbit' starts increase noise levels and waste tyres and fuel.

Example Theory Test Questions

1. You wish to leave your vehicle parked on a road. You may leave the engine switched on and running until you return:

Mark one answer

○ a. if you will only be parked for less than five minutes

○ b. to recharge a flat battery

◑ c. in no circumstances at all

○ d. if a passenger remains in the vehicle

2. When driving heavily loaded vehicles, your tyre pressures might need to be:

Mark one answer

◐ a. increased

○ b. decreased

○ c. kept the same as normal

○ d. decreased dramatically

3. If you are towing a trailer on a motorway, the maximum speed limit is:

Mark one answer

○ a. 40mph

○ b. 50mph

◑ c. 60mph

○ d. 70mph

4. You must stop if you are signalled to do so by which three of the following?

Mark three answers

○ a. pedestrian

◑ b. police officers

○ c. school-crossing patrol

○ d. a teacher accompanying children

◑ e. a red traffic light

○ f. a bus driver pulling out from a bus stop

5. On approach to a steep downhill gradient, when driving a car with automatic transmission, you should:

Mark one answer

◑ a. reduce speed so that a low gear will automatically be engaged

○ b. leave the selector in Drive and apply the foot brake

○ c. leave the selector in Drive and apply the hand brake

◑ d. reduce speed and use the selector to hold down the gear

6. When negotiating a corner in a vehicle fitted with automatic transmission, you should:

Mark one answer

○ a. slow down before the corner and accelerate gently as you turn

○ b. maintain a constant speed before, during and after the corner

○ c. 'lock up' on the approach to the corner

○ d. accelerate into the corner

7. What proportion of the carbon dioxide emitted in this country is caused by transport:

Mark one answer

○ a. one-fifth

○ b. one-quarter

○ c. one-third

○ d. one-half

8. If you apply the brakes when travelling in a straight line, the extra weight is thrown on the:

Mark one answer

○ a. front wheels

○ b. rear wheels

○ c. offside wheels

○ d. all wheels equally

9. Rounding a bend, the oil pressure warning light flickers. You should pull up as soon as safely possible on the assumption that:

Mark one answer

○ a. the oil pump has broken

○ b. the oil level in the sump is very low

○ c. the oil level in the sump is between the maximum and minimum level

○ d. the oil pressure gauge light is faulty

10. Catalytic converters reduce carbon monoxide, nitrogen oxide and hydro-carbons by up to:

Mark one answer

○ a. 50%

○ b. 60%

○ c. 70%

○ d. 90%

11. You should check the pressure of your tyres when they are:

Mark one answer

○ a. hot

○ b. cold

○ c. warm

○ d. at any temperature

12. You are carrying two 10-year-old children and their parents in your car. The responsibility for seeing that the children wear seat belts rests with:

Mark one answer

○ a. the parents of the children
○ b. the children themselves
○ c. the front-seat passengers
○ d. you the driver

13. A provisional licence to drive a car is normally valid:

Mark one answer

○ a. for 6 months
○ b. for one year
○ c. until the holder's 70th birthday
○ d. for five years

14. You should test your brakes after driving through a ford because:

Mark one answer

○ a. you would be driving on a slippery road surface
○ b. your brakes may have overheated
○ c. your brakes may be soaking wet
○ d. water will have got into the hydraulic system

15. 'Kick down' on a vehicle fitted with automatic transmission enables you to:

Mark one answer

○ a. use engine compression to assist braking
○ b. accelerate quickly with more engine power
○ c. reduce petrol consumption
○ d. charge the battery quicker

16. The MOT regulations require that once a year all cars must be tested which, from their date of registration, are:

Mark one answer

○ a. over 2 years old
○ b. over 3 years old
○ c. over 4 years old
○ d. over 5 years old

17. The number of driving offence penalty points needed for disqualification is 12 if they are accumulated over:

Mark one answer

○ a. 2 years
○ b. 3 years
○ c. 5 years
○ d. 10 years

18. You are travelling at 60mph on an empty, straight section of road. A tyre bursts and your car starts to weave. You should do two of the following things:

Mark two answers
- ◯ a. allow the car to roll slowly to a halt at the side of the road
- ◯ b. hold the steering wheel firmly to keep control
- ◯ c. apply the brakes
- ◯ d. do an emergency brake
- ◯ e. use your gears to slow down quickly

19. You are driving in foggy or misty conditions, and can see the tail lights of a vehicle ahead. You should drive at a speed so that:

Mark one answer
- ◯ a. you can overtake the car in front
- ◯ b. you can stop within the distance your headlights show to be clear
- ◯ c. you can stop before reaching the tail lights of the car in front
- ◯ d. you can just keep the tail lights within the range of your headlights

20. You feel the rear wheels of your car sliding to the right. To correct the skid you should:

Mark one answer
- ◯ a. steer to the left
- ◯ b. brake and hold the wheel firmly
- ◯ c. not turn the steering wheel
- ◯ d. steer to the right

21. You are towing a trailer and it starts to snake. You should:

Mark one answer
- ◯ a. increase speed and hold the steering wheel firmly
- ◯ b. brake hard and hold the steering wheel firmly
- ◯ c. let go of the steering wheel until it corrects itself
- ◯ d. ease off the accelerator slowly

22. It is an offence to drive a car without working lamps:

Mark one answer
- ◯ a. during the hours of darkness
- ◯ b. during daylight
- ◯ c. at any time
- ◯ d. except in an emergency

23. To provide a more efficient public transport system, and a more environmentally friendly form of transport, many large towns and cities are introducing:

Mark one answer

○ a. bus lanes
○ b. light rapid transit systems (LRT)
○ c. toll roads
○ d. communal bicycle share schemes

24. When you apply the brakes, the vehicle pulls to the left. The most likely cause is inefficient:

Mark one answer

○ a. front brakes
○ b. rear brakes
○ c. nearside brakes
○ d. offside brakes

25. You park your vehicle at the side of the road, facing uphill, you should apply the hand brake and select:

Mark one answer

○ a. fifth gear
○ b. reverse gear
○ c. neutral
○ d. first gear

26. A driver sees that the tyres of his vehicle are badly worn in the centre of the tread pattern. It is most likely that:

Mark one answer

○ a. there is too much pressure in the tyres
○ b. there is too little pressure in the tyres
○ c. this is a normal pattern of wear
○ d. the tyres are the wrong size for the vehicle

27. While driving along an open road, you notice that the temperature gauge of your vehicle is recording a rapid rise in temperature. The most likely cause of this is:

Mark one answer

○ a. the engine oil is low
○ b. the spark plugs have oiled up
○ c. the fan belt has broken
○ d. the thermostat has broken

Answers and Explanations

1. c. is correct. It is illegal to leave your vehicle with the engine running.
2. a.
3. c.
4. b. c. and e.
5. d.
6. a.
7. a.
8. a. is correct. If you brake, more weight is thrown onto the front wheels.
9. b. is correct. If the pump was broken, the warning light would stay on; so (a) is wrong. If the level was between the maximum and minimum, nothing would happen. (This is where it should be.) But if the oil level in the sump is low, the oil pressure warning light may flicker as you go around a bend. The car going round a bend 'sloshes' the oil around in the sump. When there is not enough oil over the pressure switch, it will activate the warning light. When the oil moves back over the switch again, the warning light goes out.
10. d.
11. b. Tyres get hot as you drive along and the pressure inside increases. Recommended pressures are always stated for cold tyres.
12. d. The driver is responsible for children under 14 securing their seat belts.
13. c.
14. c. You should dry out your brakes if necessary by selecting first gear and edging forwards slowly with your left foot on the brake pedal and your right foot on the accelerator.
15. b.
16. b.
17. b.
18. a. and b.
19. b.
20. d.
21. d. is correct. Any other action is likely to make matters worse.
22. c.
23. b.
24. d.
25. d.
26. a. is correct. Too much pressure leaves only the central part of the tyre in contact with the road, causing it to wear out.
27. c. is correct. The fan belt is used to drive the water pump, which sends the coolant round the engine and back to the radiator. If the coolant isn't moving, the engine cannot be cooled and will eventually boil over.

Index

£5 off your first BSM driving lesson

This voucher entitles the bearer to £5 off their first driving lesson with a BSM instructor when presented with a copy of this book.

Conditions of use: 1. The offer is for £5 off the local centre lesson price of a first one-hour learner driver lesson with a BSM instructor. 2. Applicants must hold a provisional driving licence when they take the lesson. 3. Only one voucher per person. 4. The offer is only available in mainland UK and is subject to availability. 5. There is no cash alternative. 6. The offer may not be used in conjunction with any other first lesson offer or discount from BSM.

Promoter: The British School of Motoring Limited as agent for BSM franchised instructors, 81/87 Hartfield Road, London SW19 3TJ.

To book your BSM driving lesson, please call 0345 276 276.

For BSM centre use:

PEP No. _____ Car No. _____ Centre code _____

Voucher value: £5   Date _____ BK/FL/5

BSM instructors operate under a franchise with The British School of Motoring Limited, the largest organisation of its kind in the world.